MW00834327

HERO UNAWARE

LETTERS HOME FROM A NAVY CORPSMAN DURING WWII

DOUG DODD

PUBLICATION CONSULTANTS
WE BELIEVE IN THE POWER OF AUTHORS

PO Box 221974 Anchorage, Alaska 99522-1974
books@publicationconsultants.com—www.publicationconsultants.com

ISBN Number: 978-1-63747-021-3
eBook ISBN Number: 978-1-63747-022-0

Library of Congress Number: 2021909376

Copyright 2021 Doug Dodd
—First Edition—

All rights reserved, including the right of
reproduction in any form, or by any mechanical
or electronic means including photocopying or
recording, or by any information storage or
retrieval system, in whole or in part in any
form, and in any case not without the
written permission of the author and publisher.

Manufactured in the United States of America

This book is dedicated to the Navy Corpsmen and Doctors who provided medical care for the Marines in the Pacific during World War Two.

★ ROI - NAMUR

★ SAIPAN

★ TINIAN

Base Camp
Oct 19, 1944

Dear Folks
    I'll write this note on the 4th Marines
latest job of publicity.
    Frank & I just had another
argument - he won. What is shrapnel?
He proved its the material within the
projectal rather than the shell casing.
    I received the letter saying you
received the 4 money orders & 2 package
one I'm going to open this evening
seems to be the fruit cake.
    Likely by now Dad is home
again & the next letter will tell
me about it.
    What happened to the deed I
signed - suppose it was no good.
    I guess I didn't mention it
but I'm attending school also
believe the quarter started about
10-10-44. The Regament decided

4

that their 1/c were all together too dumb so made it compulsory for them to attend optional for lower rates. So far they haven't conducted a class that has been coherent but maybe will get organized later on.

Went to town yesterday & about the only thing that I did was buy a watch band & have a rate sewed on my shirt. Its the first 1/c that I have worn altho Ive had the rate since May. Received a letter from Mannie congratulating me upon the promotion. Guess I won't tell her how long its been since she wrote.

We have another new record among others that I like. its Lili Marlene. Probably its an old piece over there.

If you can will you send me some film size 127. Zaar has a camera but very little film now. May send you a picture later.

✗ censor rule

Love,
Walter.

Walter E Dodd Ph M 1/c USNR

CONTENTS

INTRODUCTION

My father, Walter Erwin Dodd, was born October 19, 1918, in a clapboard house in Anaconda, Montana. He died ninety-eight years later on October 25, 2016, at his home in Missoula.

Like hundreds of thousands of other young men of his generation, Dad served in the military in World War II. Most of these men, boys many of them, wrote letters to their families 'back in the states.' My father was a prodigious correspondent, and after his death I was amazed to discover in his effects, a sealed box containing over three hundred wartime letters, in their original envelopes, addressed to his parents Missoula, Montana.

Growing up I knew nothing of the letters and very little about his service. I knew he had been a Navy corpsman and had served with the Marines in the Pacific. Toward the end of his life he finally began to speak about his wartime experiences which were horrific, depressing, and hilarious by turns and I began to understand why his time with the Marines had remained a closed book for so many years. The letters opened a window, not just into his life as a Navy corpsman, but also into the character of a quiet, humble, and quite remarkable man. Before I share them with you, I'd like you to meet Walter as he was before the war - before everything changed.

DISCLAIMER – I have edited quotes from Walter's letters for spelling, grammar, and punctuation. His cursive handwriting is usually quite legible, though 'O' and 'A' are sometimes a puzzle. His punctuation and spelling are mysterious and inconsistent. He uses '&' and 'and' interchangeably with '&'

being most common. With these last two, I have tried to follow his usage. When legibility becomes an issue, I make my best guess.

Walter looks happy in his Navy Blues

As a Marine – not so much.

At Camp Pendleton with other Corpsmen

PART 1 – EARLY LIFE IN MONTANA
OCTOBER 19, 1918 – JANUARY 1, 1942

Walter's mother, Myrtle Chilcote, was born 1894 in Missoula, Montana where she lived out her first eight years with her parents, Charlie, and Jessie Chilcote. In 1902 Charlie moved his growing family – Jessie eventually gave birth to nine children - twelve miles north of Missoula to a place on Butler Creek. The place was never solely farm or ranch, but always a little of both. Call it what you will, it was steeped in failure. The largest part, section 17, was only leased with option to buy – if they could keep up the annual payments. The two smaller parcels were homesteads where other families had tried and failed. Myrtle remained on Butler Creek with her parents till 1917 when she married Albert Dodd.

When they married their prospects seemed bright. Al was a foreman for the Anaconda Copper Mining Company at the smelter in their eponymous company town in western Montana. Myrtle was a five-foot dynamo who could, and usually did, outwork most men. If Al could just bring home a regular paycheck, Myrtle would build a good life for him and the children she hoped to bear. But the deck was stacked against them from the start.

Copper was King in Montana. The ACM rigged elections, bribed legislators, hired goons to assault organizers, labeled unions as communist, suborned judges, controlled the press, and owned much of the land. Because of the smelter, the entire town – the water, the earth, the very air – was high in cyanide, mercury, lead, and other heavy metals. Plants, animals, and people sickened and died in the toxic stew, imprisoned by their dependence on the ACM for their income. Walter was less than a year old when Al became too ill to work at the smelter.

Al struggled with decisions and sometime chose badly. He never found another paying job he wanted to keep, so for the next twelve years the family moved, first to Missoula, then to Idaho, held together by Myrtle's frugality, hard work, prolific gardens, and indomitable will.

Meanwhile, back on Butler Creek, Charlie had been driving his boys mercilessly to make the place a success. Unfortunately, after Charlie died in 1923, the boys did not want to harness teams of work horses, plow fields and cut hay. The ranch began a slow downhill slide and when the Depression hit in 1929, the 'hill' became a precipice. By the time Jessie died in December of 1930, the place was in ruins. Myrtle's brothers had sold the livestock and any of the machinery that hadn't already broken down. By then the hay fields had returned to cheat and quack grasses and could barely support a few cows and horses.

Myrtle returned from Idaho and somehow cajoled her siblings into ceding her their shares in the failing ranch. On April 1, 1931, Myrtle, and her family, now grown to four with the birth of her second son, took possession of Butler Creek.

Picture Walter's life that April Fool's Day. Not yet thirteen, he would have seen a ramshackle house, two doorless log barns, mostly empty of livestock, a few small, weathered sheds, with the whole shebang surrounded by a few derelict automobiles and obsolete horse drawn machinery. There was no running water or electricity and Butler Creek, one hundred fifty feet below the house, was the sole source of water. The place sat at the end of a narrow, rutted road, three miles from their nearest neighbors. It is hard to overstate the isolation, poverty, and primitive conditions on the place where, in the depths of the Great Depression, Walter spent the next ten years.

Any ranch, and especially one in need of rehabilitation, is all about work, and here all the work had to be done by hand. They grew most of their food, and Myrtle planted a large garden. She managed to acquire some chickens, a pig, and a milk cow. When they could afford it, they bought chicken feed in fifty-pound cloth sacks. Myrtle made the sacks into towels, sheets and even dresses for herself. She was a persuasive speaker and a great storyteller. People were attracted to her and in another life, she could have run for office – and won. Failure for Myrtle, on the ranch or in life, was never an option.

Of Walter's many jobs his first year on the ranch, the most onerous was hauling water. All Myrtle's projects, cooking, cleaning, washing clothes, and raising chickens, required water. The garden required more water than all the other projects combined, and Walter hauled it all. For their household needs he carried water from the creek a hundred and fifty feet up the hill to the big wooden barrel that sat by the wood-burning cook stove in the kitchen. Sometimes he used metal five-gallon buckets, and other times five or ten-gallon milk cans; either way, a gallon weighed 8.34 pounds and the barrel probably held fifty-five gallons or 458 pounds. In the summer, counting the house and garden, he likely made at least seventy-five trips a day with a bucket in each hand. Even allowing for spillage, that would have amounted to over three tons of water every day. No wonder, when I asked him eighty years later, how he felt about his time as a water boy, he said flatly, "I was her slave."

Myrtle and Al were very different. Neither was well educated but Myrtle was intelligent and sought to increase her knowledge. I remember when I was eight or ten, we used to memorize Readers Digest vocabulary words together. She also had a knowledge of the bible, probably from her early Methodist upbringing. She loved hymns and 'What a Friend We Have in Jesus' was her favorite. Although it was impractical for her to attend church, she listened to the Old-Fashioned Revival Hour on an old battery powered Motorola and kept a book of daily devotions by her chair. She believed in hard work, wouldn't abide drinking or swearing, and believed God didn't approve of miscegenation. She didn't like wars but thought they were sometimes unavoidable.

Albert smoked a pipe as well as tailor-mades when he could get them, and to my knowledge didn't drink or swear. He articulated no specific religious or political beliefs, though Time magazine was a kind of Gospel, with FDR cast as Lucifer. He distained unions, especially the 'I won't work' I.W.W.

From 1931 to 1936, if Walter wasn't working or sleeping, he was probably in school – the only regular activity that freed him temporarily from the grip the ranch had on his life. Walter started high school in Missoula in the fall of '32, twelve miles away. During blizzards which could last for a week, he might board in Missoula with Neil Dahlstrom, a fellow student and cousin by marriage. It was the beginning of a friendship that lasted over seventy years.

By the time Walter was a junior he was sixteen and a licensed driver. Judging by his report cards from his last three years, Walter was a B - minus student, not bad considering his endless chores at home and his imperfect attendance. Studying by dim, smokey kerosene lamps couldn't have helped. He was well behaved, and four teachers complimented him on his attitude, two on his social consciousness, and one each on his initiative and his improvement.

A perceptive admissions officer from, say, Montana State College in Bozeman, meeting Walter at his high school graduation in 1936, would have seen a quiet, motivated, above average student. He didn't drink, smoke, or swear, he was courteous to his peers, and willing to work hard. A closer look would have revealed Walter's strong desire to study agriculture in college.

By today's standards he might be considered deserving of a scholarship because of his family's low income, but that was not to be in the 30's. The nation remained mired in the Great Depression, and Walter's time and very body were necessary for the ranch to survive. Besides a few cash jobs, he worked the next five years on the ranch, where they lived hand to mouth, day by day, month by month, until December 7, 1941, when the world came to Walter. This is how he remembered it.

"We didn't hear about the attack right away, until one of the neighbors, I can't remember who, came up with a paper and talked to Mother. No one knew what would happen and she was worried. We heard rumors; some people thought the Japs might land on the west coast or bomb Seattle. A lot of the family was in Washington. If I had to go, what would happen to the ranch?"

He had already registered with the Selective Service, and on September 30 the local board classified him 1-A. He must have appealed almost immediately, because on November 3 he received notice his appeal was denied. Myrtle disagreed. After all, wasn't farming an occupation critical to the nation?

Walter felt torn. His family needed him, but the papers told him the country needed him too, and with his appeal denied, the choice was out of his hands. That year Christmas for the family was bleaker than usual. Besides his family's usual poverty, Walter was pessimistic about his future if he were drafted. He described it to me like this:

"I thought that if I were drafted into the army I'd probably be killed or even worse, maimed for life. It occurred to me that if I went in the Navy and my ship was torpedoed, at least it would be over all at once. I was really confused, and Mother was too upset to discuss it. I remember a day or two after Christmas, it was cold with just a little snow. Pop and Mother had gone to town. After I finished my chores, I walked up the canyon to the old orchard. It felt even colder there, and I just walked back and forth talking – I'm not sure who I was talking to. We didn't go to church and I didn't really know how to pray. I wanted to know what to do. All at once, this great warm feeling came over me and I wasn't afraid. I knew what I had to do, and I was at peace."

The following Monday, December 29, 1941 Walter went to Missoula and volunteered for service in the U.S. Navy. He was not alone. Many other Montana boys also volunteered, among them Neil Dahlstrom who Walter had boarded with in high school. Unlike Walter, Neil had enrolled that fall at Montana State University in Missoula but had withdrawn after Pearl Harbor. Now Neil and Walter found themselves together again. The physical exam and pages of forms took three days, and on January 1, Walter enlisted in the US Navy for a period of two years.

PART 2 – SAN DIEGO – 28 LETTERS
JANUARY 1, 1942 – MARCH 23, 1942

Walter's first letter, January 2, sent from Salt Lake City, is on stationary from The Wilson, Hotel and Apartments. There he and about a hundred other recruits are housed as they wait to be assigned. He begins with "Dear Folks" and the date and closes with "Love Walter." He follows this pattern in nearly every letter. This short letter is mostly about the weather and the train trip. "It was certainly some ride down here. Leaving Butte, the track began to get rough. Even the brake man couldn't hardly walk down the aisle.... When they would back up and jerk, they hit the cars so hard it almost hurt a person...." – but contains little significant information and ends with a cryptic "Will be here 5 days. Perhaps." This long train trip is just the first of uncountable new experiences.

Walter begins his letter of January 5 with a short weather report and then describes "the Mormon block." He is clearly impressed by the Tabernacle and Dome "...three arches one over the other and braced & fixed solid so that it's 11ft. thru. The dome has no pillars or supports, Seats 8,000, 11,000 standing room.... made of stone hauled from the mountains, took 40 years to build& cost a little less than $4,000,000 dollars."

The final page details the recruit's daily schedule almost to the minute. He closes with the observation that "Hickox and Morrison have been out the last few nights, so they sleep most of the afternoon.... Love Walter U.S.N."

By January 9, the five day stay Walter expected has become a week and he is tired of "…all the drunks, idiots and salty slush on the streets."

In San Diego on January 14, Walter and Neil are assigned to the same barracks. Since it holds 2,000 men that isn't surprising, but Walter is pleased their bunks are close together. Perhaps their proximity is due to the Navy's apparent fondness for alphabetical ordering. Even with 2,000 names, Dahlstrom and Dodd are not that far apart.

Walter itemizes everything. Clothing - T-shirt, work pants, wool sweater, watch cap, and "My blue dress suit (which) fits well." Weather - "clear but seems strange." Life insurance - "I took out $5,000 at $3.30 per month $.66 on the thousand." The return of his civilian gear - "We had to send our clothing C.O.D. because they didn't have time…otherwise. I kept my shoes as …we didn't know when we would be issued more." The food - "…good but they dish out too much. I miss the milk."

On January 21, Walter writes for the first time in a week. He has been busy, what with the daily "policing and swabbing the deck, - sweeping and mopping the floor." He has also unpacked, folded and distributed clothing to "…recruits until 2200. I never opened so many boxes before in all my life."

He has taken tests to qualify for "some school…very limited space in the schools…I'm quite sure I won't make one." His pessimism is understandable, and indeed his test scores are merely average. However, we can make allowances; he has had a reaction to one of the vaccinations, either the smallpox or the typhoid, and is writing from sick bay, in pencil, and on borrowed paper, where he still has a very sore arm and a fever. He devotes the bulk of the letter to family news and then closes as follows: "One of our co. was thrown in the brig. Rumor has it he deserted the army. I saw him in S.L. and didn't like him. Left him talking. Feeling fine. Don't worry. Love Walter Erwin Dodd U.S. Naval Training Station, San Diego, Cal."

By January 23, Walter is out of sick bay after just 30 hours. He still has a cold which he blames on the weather. "The climate is so damp it's like working in a room where someone is doing a washing…" He received no mail while in Salt Lake and now his mother's letters, apparently filled with questions, have finally caught up with him. The result is this rambling letter, wherein he provides a detailed critique of his gear and clothing, from the unhemmed cuffs on his jacket to the fact that his stationary gets crumpled in his ditty bag. Eventually he will adjust to the vagaries of Naval mail service.

Over the next page he delivers a mishmash of one-liners on unrelated subjects. He is pleased his brother Byron shot a coyote that was after their sheep. Walter has decided not to spend $1.75 for a picture of himself to send home. "…you know what I look like anyway." He bemoans the rainy weather, and frets about the near impossibility of being accepted into any Navy school.

Most of the daily duty is easy for him, not surprising since he has ranch work for comparison. "It is very hard on young fellows 17 &18. They can't quiet down and obey rules. They get on the bad list. It doesn't seem the place for a boy until about 20. As a whole I like the fellows here. A couple I passively dislike & 2 actively. We don't have trouble but that's all. Mr. Reese, our commanding officer, is very nice. He doesn't swear at us as some officers do at their companies. I hate to hear them drilling their outfits."

Walter describes the entertainment provided for the men: free movies every night, which he often skips, and two upcoming stage shows by big name stars. One is by Burns and Allen, that very afternoon and another by Bob Hope the following week which he expects to miss because the scuttlebutt has the company moving out before then.

His new life, noisy, crowded, and regimented, is the opposite of the ranch. A 'boy' could be overwhelmed but Walter resolves to stand firm. To avoid being corrupted, and perhaps as reassurance to his mother, he writes: "The fellows, free, happy, & young, use an awful lot of strong language. In order to keep from following suit, I don't even use slang. I'm surely glad I don't smoke too. Some fellows can't hardly stand a four-hr. watch without a cigarette."

Walter begins his January 26 letter with excitement. "Dear Folks— Boy, oh Boy!! I saw Bob Hope broadcast tonight over N.B.C. Was that something. He came on …before the program and then for 10 or 12 minutes after. On the cast were Betty Hutton, a painted doll, but boy could she sing and perform…. It was just fortunate that I got to go. Only 97 men from our company were allowed to go. I wasn't picked (but) because I had done the duties around the barracks, he (the Chief Petty Officer) put my name on in place of some who were sick. He & I get on swell." Walter is ignoring the enlisted man's axiom to 'never volunteer for anything,' and, so far, is reaping the rewards.

Sometimes it seems he is trying to record everything – a clear impossibility – which gives his letters an almost telegraphic style. "Today was a busy day. I had to get up at 3:30 to go on guard duty. It's 8:30 now – they're taking Jensen out on a stretcher, passed out. Today a fellow committed suicide across the parade grounds. Slashed his throat and wrists." I imagine a story like this would 'worry Myrtle no end.' What must San Diego be like if young men are committing suicide?

Walter continues with trivia. "At 6:30 they lined up for chow & at 7:30 went over for our pay check; came back and paid our bills." Walter's world is upside down, the ranch is already becoming a fading memory, his future is uncertain, and it is hard for him to know which events are newsworthy.

It is soon apparent that their letters often pass each other in the mail. Myrtle saved each of Walter's letters, most in the original envelope, so we can see from the postmarks that first class mail from the San Diego Naval Hospital took about two weeks to reach Missoula. Al and Myrtle will later rent a P.O. box in Missoula, but at this time their mail arrived general delivery. They usually picked up mail every Friday, so it might be up to three weeks before they actually opened a letter. Until he went into combat, Walter seldom went one week, and never two, without writing home. Judging by his references to his mother's letters (none of which he was able to save due to space constraints and regulations) she often repeats questions he believes he has already answered.

The ranch will not have phone service till after the war, so letters are their only link. Right now, delayed mail is merely annoying. Later, after Walter goes into combat, it will become a source of deep anxiety for Myrtle and even cause Walter to refuse a medal. But that will come later.

"January 28, noon I feel fine; was working over in the carpentry shop sweeping up the floor whenever anyone finished with a machine, no work lots of fun. Must have done OK because he said to be sure to come back if I were sent on a work party this P.M. I should have written sooner but I'm answering two at once now." The rest of his letter is spent answering concerns his family, mostly Myrtle, must have raised in her letters.

January 30th "Dear Folks, in a hurry again but I've got good news. I made the medical school!! Didn't expect to after I saw my grades and saw the list of men to go to the schools." Walter's excitement is clear, and I wonder what other opportunities he has had to measure himself against other young men. Isolated on the ranch, he never participated in any extracurricular sports or scholastic activities, never joined 4-H or FFA (Future Farmers of America), and as far as I have been able to discover, never participated in any organized competition with his fellows. The ranch has taught him to work hard at any task and now we see that his ability exceeds his confidence.

The rest of his letter is anticlimactic, and Walter closes with a description of his new dog tags. "Two stainless steel oval shaped pieces of metal about the size of a ½ dollar with our full name, blood type, serial no. (mine's 660 10 78) and USNR stenciled on the front and our right index finger print on the back. We also carry an identification card with our picture (looks like that of a convict), signature, finger print and states on mine that it will be void Jan. 1, 1946. We wear our dog tags around our neck on a cloth-covered wire." His letter then jumps suddenly to a complaint about the bitterness of Navy coffee. I wonder, did Walter belatedly realize that a main purpose of dog tags is to facilitate the identification of corpses, and not wanting to alarm his family, is he suddenly desperate to change the subject?

By the end of January, Walter has written ten letters home and an unknown number of others to relatives and friends. His descriptions, whether about his dog tags, the weather, his clothing, the barracks, or the landscape, are very detailed. He seems fascinated and curious about everything.

His emotions are another matter. I re-read his letters, searching for clues as to his thoughts and find ...almost nothing. The words are there:

"I'm fine… sorry to hear about Donald… Boy oh boy, good news! … Love, Walter" and he seems sincere, but I cannot tell how Walter feels.

His brother David recalls that "Mother told that in one of the first letters she wrote to him she described how pretty the cold and frost on the trees made the ranch look. She said he asked her not to describe things like that because it made him homesick."

Writing February 1, Walter notes that a couple of his folks' letters have arrived via Salt Lake. Walter has already answered some of their questions, but to be safe he answers them again. That done, he continues "I will start school Feb. 9 according to plans. I still can't believe it." Already life on the ranch is starting to feel far away as he notes: "Strange I'd almost forgotten the dogs' names."

Walter, unimpressed by Navy weaponry, reveals a talent for mockery: "Our rifles are 30/06 carbines, old World War variety. They're no good as far as guns are concerned but more impressive than a broom stick. We have no target practice. Very little drill so far 4 or 5 days. Most of our time seems to be taken up in the chow line. That's harder than real work."

Walter enclosed a note to his brother David who would have been not quite seven. Written in cursive as though to an adult, it describes the local flora and concludes with "When mother calls you to dinner be sure and hurry. You don't know the privilege. Here we have to stand in line all the way from 5 min to 1 hr. & 15 min. I hope you still like school, David. Goodbye, Walter."

In his letter of February 4 he describes what he saw after the company's three-mile march to the zoo. "I think we saw all of the animals but not…the ostriches. We were too tired…. We didn't hardly ever stop and often ran…. It's the first time I ever saw a gorilla. Boy could he ever sit back and stare…. They put on a trained seal show and a bear act…. A person could spend a long time in there." But his mood is broken when "Hudson, one of the worst guys in our company threw a box into the bear pen…. Hudson is about thirty, dark, squat built, who thinks he's a prize fighter. Just noise. Some of the fellows in our company although old enough in age act very childish. Six or eight spoil the whole company and we've got the reputation of being the worst in camp…. Some Rep, eh?"

Done venting, Walter closes on a positive note. "I have no picture of David and would like for you to send me one when you can, otherwise I guess I'm satisfied as could be expected. Love, Walter."

On February 5, Walter, Neil and about 160 other recruits begin classes in the San Diego USN HCS (United States Navy Hospital Corpsman School). "Dear Mom & family, Well I did make it. I'm in the hospital school grounds…. This building we're using has a new head put in but still not enough hot water. Gee, I'm glad to get away from the last barracks, just 66 men sleep in this room. Makes it quiet…. Oh boy, the beds. They (are) 36" wide at least and have good mattresses on them. Also, sheets."

Walter asks about the ranch's herd of Columbia sheep. "Gee I hope the lamb crop is heavy, also that the ewes have plenty of milk, are they in good condition?"

"I've been very sick… I reported to sick bay…. Had quite a fever…. They gave me medicine & told me to stay in bed…. Had chills much of the time. Wed night I was very sick fever was so high I couldn't hardly see. I was out of my head part of the night. Up till midnight I couldn't sleep, chills and severe pain in my right lung." Walter's list of symptoms goes on, first to dizziness, then to a deep cough and finally to a throat that "bleeds something fierce." Walter returns to duty a day or so later even though "… my nose & throat are running blood, but I seem to feel good."

This last paragraph was not written by the Walter I knew. Myrtle would already be on tenterhooks about the many dangers awaiting Walter in the war, and this letter surely worried her. I never saw Dad exaggerate his health problems, usually the opposite was true, so perhaps he was too ill to hide his real condition. After an additional half page of inconsequential remarks, he closes with "Feel fine – love Walter."

Through the first half of February letters to Walter roll in. Besides two or three every week from his family, undoubtedly written by Myrtle, he mentions receiving mail from Aunt Sjaan, and Cousin Vera. Walter gives as good as he gets. In the first ten days of February, he composes five letters home and covers eleven full sized pages. On February 12 he receives two letters and takes the time from his studies to write again.

"Boy, yesterday I felt homesick and tired of it all. Today the letters helped, and I just feel like letting some things slide. My class notes are supposed to be ready for inspection tomorrow. Must be in ink but the ship store doesn't have any. I borrowed this pencil so I could save ink."

As he continues, I see flashes of his wry humor. "Tomorrow they may have ink & pencils, today they have candy and soap." Already that morning he has had classes on nursing, diagnosis and litter carrying. "In the afternoon we start with bandaging, few notes but much practice. Then a class on Anatomy, Physiology, and Osteology." The instructor "... is good but tough. Knows all bones, tissues, organs, functions, spelling, and everything.... 206 bones to remember. I don't know if I can do it or not. I'll try. If we are good enough, we get a choice of where we'll be stationed. Bremerton is on the list."

Walter and Myrtle know Bremerton would be his first choice. He has cousins, aunts, and uncles in western Washington, and if he is stationed there, he will manage to see them.

Walter raises the subject of money and his pay. "I can leave my money here with the gov't and draw interest until discharged. I had intended for you to use the money I can spare though. Glad to hear you have a market for mutton, a few more and you can sell all the cull ewes."

Walter responds to the death of a neighboring rancher: "Really sorry about Mr. M. I suppose she will sell the place.... Really too bad. Seems like such a short time ago that I saw him.... Must close no more time must get notes in order & copied in ink. Love, Walter Erwin Dodd"

February 15, 1942 – "Dear Mom and Family, I don't know why I'm writing, just am, I guess. I had my first liberty last night.... from 5pm to midnight. Neil and I went downtown on the streetcar.... We were paid yesterday. He and I each received $10. I don't believe I'll send any home this time I'll have my tooth fixed first.... We ate a meal 46 cent special.... I don't like San Diego. The sidewalks are narrow & traffic is heavy. The town is jammed with sailors, Marines, and soldiers, in that order. You see very few civilians, and the women we've seen so far are terrible in looks and actions. An awful lot of Mexican and Negroes. Most people are dark complected."

The rest of the letter is largely about the myriad rules and information a new corpsman must master. What with memorizing every bone in the human body, drilling repeatedly on bandaging and litter carrying, and at the end of each day cleaning the makeshift classrooms, Walter has been too busy to go to church or read the *Saturday Evening Post*.

The men don't have lockers, but they still must keep all their gear neatly stowed, their shoes shined, hair cut to regulation, and uniforms laundered, pressed, and in good repair. Possession of stolen property results in a court martial, and this rule is interpreted to cover clothing which is marked with someone else's initials, so borrowing, or even lending, a shirt or cap is a risk.

Walter signs off after three and a half gloomy pages and then uses a postscript to add a little more negative news. "A bottle of liquor was found in the head this A.M." An offense punishable by court martial, of course. He follows that with "…a boy fell down a stairs & has a fractured skull." Almost out of space, and perhaps conscious of his letter's negative tone, Walter closes his letter on a lighter note. "They have a Coke machine in our barracks. They empty it every day… Love, Walter."

By Sunday, February 22, Walter has received two new letters from home and his mood has brightened considerably. On his most recent liberty, he bought an Easterbrook fountain pen for $0.75 and this letter is in ink.

His health has improved. "I can smell, taste and hear normally now, first time since I came down here." His moral is good, buoyed by corpsman's school. "Somehow, I don't mind it so much here now; something worthwhile to do, good (swell) food, good beds, and I believe a better class of fellows as a whole than in our company. You know now I have no connections with the old company."

Myrtle has reported that a brutal cold snap has hit during lambing season. "I wish I were there to help out with the lambing… how cold did it get at the worst? Doesn't bother me any to talk about it from here; bananas and avocados on the trees, spring planting editions in the papers and … last night it rained."

Walter is deeply involved in his training. "I've been here two weeks now, tests next week. Doesn't seem possible. I've been so busy it took me three days to read the paper I bought…. I wasn't marked as an awkward in litter drill yesterday as some were."

Even busy, Walter finds time for a variety of activities, though once again he skips church. "The bleachers will be too wet for me to go." On liberty, the day before, he saw a civilian dentist who filled a cavity for $5.50. Then Walter splurged for a leather notebook, complete with pencil, paper and eraser, a $1.51 purchase.

Toward the end of his four-page letter, he confesses to volunteering for extra guard duty because … "I generally wake up during the night and lay awake. This morning I woke up at 4:00 and didn't go back to sleep." He repeats a familiar complaint about the immaturity of the other recruits. "Sometimes I wonder if the fellows here are boys or men. Some of the classes here tear up each other's bed, and hang them from the rafters, play around and don't learn their lessons…. Think I'll wash and go to bed. Note new address. Love Walter Erwin Dodd, Company 4, US Navy Hospital Corps School, San Diego, Calif."

When he writes on February 26 the weather is moderate, the food is good, and Walter's studies are progressing. Sailors still get drunk and cause trouble. Walter stands guard duty, awaits promotion, and wonders where he will go next. Walter is adapting. He decides to give the city another chance. "I was sort of hasty in my conclusion of San Diego. It was a Sat. evening before. It was the class of people that made it so bad. I don't think I'll go down again on Sat. Wed. it looked much better although not as nice as Salt Lake or Missoula." Later he writes, "On liberty day I'm going back to the zoo, also the museum which is just two blocks up."

In Walter's new world, where mopping the floor is swabbing the deck, food is chow and rumors are scuttlebutt, language itself is turned topsy-turvy. The Navy seems to love acronyms, and technical medical terms creep into his letters. In a world where "G.W. Jones, Lt. C., (MC)? USNR (PBB)" is either a description of Walter's C.O. or some mad typist's error, it should come as no surprise when Walter's self-imposed decision to refrain from using slang breaks down. How is he supposed to know that 'pogey bait' (in all its several spellings) is not an innocent term for candy and/or cigarettes? With luck, Myrtle will not be able to determine this term's various meanings.

Walter is excited about all he is learning in corpsman training. He can name the 206 bones in the body and his test scores are good. He has high expectations for himself even though almost everyone else has had some previous training such as "… premed courses, 1-3 years, Red Cross courses, experience in hospitals and undertaking parlors, etc. I'm going to try to be in the first 25 of my class though. They get to choose their hospital to work in. Bremerton is one of the choices." Bremerton, at least for the time, has become Walter's North Star and his assignment there will depend on his performance in corpsman school.

Looking back, on January 21, he took the Navy GCT to determine if he even qualified for one of the Navy 'Schools.' That day, after scoring an 80, he wrote "I'm quite sure I won't make one." Yet now, a month later, he is competing successfully against men with previous medical training. Is it any wonder that every day the ranch seems farther away from Walter's world?

"Dear Folks, March 1, that means I've been in the service for two months. It seems so long and yet the time has flown…. The last two days I've hardly done a thing. We took a test Sat. morning right after our nursing class and were paid in the afternoon. Right now 1:00P.M. I'm lying on the lawn soaking up some very nice sunshine." Walter's nursing grades are impressive – "…96 on the test, 90 in bed making and 95 in my notes. That makes an average of 94." After a brief nod to modesty, "Not so good compared to some," he points out that two more experienced men had lower scores.

Now that he has a little free time, he spends a page discussing the finer points of military grooming such as shoe shining and how to get his whites really clean.

Walter mentions receiving two letters from Elsie, a package from Aunt Sjaan and one letter each from two other female relatives, Vera, and Lena. Aunt Sjaan wants him to write to "Betty", which Walter finds amusing. (David explained that "Aunt Sjaan had designs on Walter as a husband for her niece Betty from the time they were very young and made no bones about her wishes.")

Walter asks briefly about the health of three neighbors and the sheep. The neighbors all have names, but the sheep he identifies by number. "We should have killed no. 15 last fall. I suppose 19, 11, 16, 7, & perhaps 45 will have to go soon. Under the circumstances sounds like lambing is coming fine the twins aren't plentiful enough to pay for the oats, are they?

"Gee the girls that hang around here are disgusting. Neil says there are no good ones here. I tell him that we only see the scum because we don't get around. Here they are called San Quentin Quail. Very suggestive…. If I keep on, I'll have to put on an extra stamp. Send me all the news and don't work too hard. I'm fine and hope you all are too. PS. Send my love to Betty-via Aunt Sjaan! ha ha."

"March 4, Dear Folks—I received your letter today and tell David he wrote a swell letter. Byron will have to take some notes from him."

While almost none of the letters Walter received have been preserved, there is one exception, a half page letter from his brother David, then about seven, labeled 'March' without day or year. The content suggests that it arrived with Myrtle's letter of March 1. As Walter struggles through Corpsman School, David offers this bit of advice, "I hope you study hard. I do. With love. David Dodd." Somehow, out of all the letters he has received over four years, Walter has managed to preserve this one, which is something of a miracle, and speaks to his closeness to David. When I spoke with David, he described Walter as "more of a father figure than a brother," perhaps because of the seventeen-year difference in their ages.

Walter's March 4 letter continues, "This is our liberty night, but I didn't leave. It always costs something, and I decided to catch up on my notes. In B-2 now and they are crowding us full force. 7 periods a day, 2 of nursing…yesterday I gave and received a hypodermic…. Tell David I'm studying as I never have before." It is hard to track Walter's progress. He has yet to mention his rank or hint at the duration of his training. Does he even know? His exam scores are still good – 94 in practical nursing and 97 in anatomy – but he is not satisfied.

Continuing his letter, the next morning Walter reveals his worries about the farm. Apparently, Byron is contemplating leaving, whether to school, for a job, or just to get away Walter does not say. "How can Pop do the work if Byron goes on? Do you think you can get a hired man? In another month I can send a little more home to help pay…if you can get one. The farm is too much for one I know…. You have done very well in saving all that you have. How many cows are you milking? Not much milk I suppose, now…. Love to all Walter." Although Walter opens his letters "Dear Folks" it seems that everything of importance is directed toward his mother. Myrtle is like gravity, holding the place together with her work and her will. But Byron, 18, is restless with big dreams, and if Byron leaves, Walter fears for the farm and his parents.

Walter loves his mother, but he is helpless in the grip of the Navy. Now while other young men become proficient with guns, grenades, and other machines of war, Walter studies the human body and practices the 'field expedient' techniques he will need to use when he is deployed. At night, in the early morning, when he wakes and can't return to sleep, he must have worries. Whatever they are, they seldom appear in his letters.

March 6 – "Today they took blood donations at the hospital and … I volunteered but they didn't call my name…. They were saying they needed 50 more from B company…. Some of the fellows passed out from the effects, probably mostly mental although it does make them weak."

Walter confesses to second thoughts about Finnegan, an Irish- Russian boy he has mentioned twice before. On February 22 Walter introduced "Poor Finnegan, who complains loudly about being ordered instead of asked to do things." In a March 3 letter, he mentions that Finnegan "can't keep his voice down when arguing which is all of the time." Now, on the 6th after Finnegan participated in another argument, this one about religion, Walter writes, "He is called dumb by some and calls himself dumb, but you have to admit he uses what he has got to a good advantage. The only thing is he talks too much and too loudly. Good fellow though." Perhaps Walter is beginning to put aside some of the ethnic and religious prejudices he has learned.

He closes with, "Hope you are all well now, Pop and everyone else too. Love Walter" and I realize again that these letters are really just directed to Myrtle. Walter may urge David to do his schoolwork and admonish Byron to fill the icehouse with blocks of ice for the summer but every real question, 'How are the lambs doing? Will the hay last until spring?' Those and all questions of etiquette are intended solely for his mother. I can picture Pop in his chair, fussing with his pipe, fingering the letters, and then setting them aside.

On Monday, March 9, Walter writes, "I just got off guard duty. Roving guard at night and on Sundays has about 10 men, but today I covered the ground alone." After spending a page describing a visit to the family of one of his friends, he continues with "Just found out that I must go to early chow, just got off guard and must go back from 6 – 8. I'm tired." The next morning, after mentioning the excellent musical talents of some of the men, he drops the bad news. "No more weekend liberties here now. We have been able to get 36 hrs. of liberty but last Sun night 15 fellows on special liberty came in overleave, 3 from our class. They just stated they would grant no more."

There follows an implied weather report - "I am peeling from sunburn." - and a new Finnegan episode. "He and another boy were cleaning up the nurses' head and a nurse came in. He looked at her, she looked at him and finally it dawned on him what was wanted. He said without thinking 'Do you want us to leave?' She left. Boy did we laugh the way he tells it on himself." Walter closes with a comment about his studies. "We took a test in nursing today. Seemed so simple I wonder what the catch was…. Love Walter E. Dodd"

The next day, March 10, Walter writes again. After wishing Pop a happy 54th birthday, he describes his first blood donation. "My color is still very good. Maybe it will lower my blood pressure; it's a little high." Walter has learned a new word which he then proudly spells, "sphygmomanometer – some word, eh? It is a blood pressure testing apparatus. We had to learn that and others for nursing…. For anatomy today we must know the digestion of foods, the juices, the reactions etc."

Another recruit who failed to return from leave on time has been removed from class. "It isn't very nice to say, but I'm glad he is going. He was very slow and didn't pay attention, always complaining. Two more out of our class and it will be almost perfect. Well think I'll study a while."

Walter is always finishing or about to start studying. What drives him? Is it just the prospect of being assigned to Bremerton? Perhaps it is the prospect of a promotion and pay raise? Does he want the approval of his instructors? Could it be patriotism? He recognizes the threat Japan poses to the country, but never shows an aggressive war-spirit. Considering Walter's modest high school marks, his performance now is amazing. Of course, high school was always secondary to his duties on the farm, and now school and learning have become his duties and he appears to be thriving. Has he discovered the joy of learning?

So far Walter's life in the Navy resembles what he might have experienced in a military prep school. His main study is medicine, not war, and though he has handled and used a few firearms, the great majority of his effort is directed toward healing, not destroying. There are rules, and discipline must be maintained, and while a corpsman can be 'expelled' from school, withdrawing from the Navy is definitely not allowed. Corpsman training does have one advantage over civilian schooling. Instead of tuition, the Navy pays Walter and throws in board and room. It is not a bad deal – so far.

Friday, March 13, 1942, "Dear Folks, well today, this afternoon at 4:30 we found out that we would get our final exams tomorrow and graduate Thursday going probably to San Diego hospital for transfer from there. Everyone is very noisy & nerves on edge. Very few like the idea of missing the 3 weeks of school…. Sure made Neil mad not to be prepared for the news, guess he doesn't know he's in the Navy yet."

This is big news for these young men. They have grown to know each other and are used to a predictable daily routine. Now, sooner than they expected, they will be reassigned. Some will remain in San Diego; some will head north to Alaska and several will proceed to Bremerton. A few may end up on submarines. With their training cut short they will still be expected to treat real patients with real injuries and diseases. Neil's anger is understandable, yet Walter finds his reaction amusing. "May write more Sunday. I think I'll cram for the test. Love Walter"

When Walter writes again on March 16 now nearly all the tests are completed and graded. No matter how well he does, Walter is never completely satisfied. "I got 98. Several received 100 though.... It's been raining here the last day or so also in the barrack. Our barrack leaks so badly we can hardly find room for the beds, otherwise it's the best one."

After testing, some of the men were granted liberty. "Many of the fellows in B-4 came back drunk & messed up the place.... Seems like that's all they want liberty for." As he awaits transfer, Walter makes a rare comment on the military situation. "Certainly looks bad in the Far East. We'd better get started pretty soon." The war news is nearly all bad and Japan looks to be winning on air, land and at sea. In the past month Japan has sunk the US Carrier Langley and the Battleship Houston, driven General MacArthur out of the Philippines, and conducted a huge air raid on Darwin, Australia. In one four-day period, the Dutch on Java surrender, the British evacuate Rangoon in Burma, and the Japanese bomb Pearl Harbor again.

All the men may soon be risking their lives, and many had specific plans and prospects which have been altered by the war. Neil wants to marry as soon as possible, while Davis "... has a very steady girl. He's buying a '41 Chevrolet and plans on buying a home." For Walter, the war is something like a risky opportunity. His prospects for a financially successful life on the family's hardscrabble farm were bleak, and Walter's loyalty and sense of obligation to his mother would have sentenced him to the farm for life. Now other possibilities can open. Walter has shown himself to be an excellent student. If he survives the war, perhaps he can continue in the Navy or even go to college.

Walter's letter jumps from the proper dosage of various medicines, to rumors of a fire in a Missoula department store, to the myriad serious dangers of even a routine surgery. He touches on guard duty, last night's menu, and the happy news that his shoes are so shiny he can see his face reflected in them. He wonders if he might be transferred to Alaska, offers critiques of several non-commissioned officers, and resolves to take the test for HA1/c as soon as possible. I think he mentions sheep in there somewhere, along with a typewriter he'd like to get his hands on. All this, mind you, in three pages. As a measure of his distraction, rather than ending with his customary "Love Walter" he simply writes, "Well guess I'll close for this time."

The Navy's service school records show Walter graduated from HCS on March 19. As of that date, Walter is no longer a Sea2c (seaman second class) but a HA2c (Hospital attendant second class). Their planned eight weeks of training lasted six.

Walter's next letter, dated March 20, is typed on 5" X 7" stationary bearing the USO insignia. "Dear Folks, Boy Oh Boy, I made Bremerton.... My average grade for the six weeks was 94.6...I could have had any of the places including Florida. My place in the hospital today was the surgery no. 2. The hottest in the country... because there are so many operations performed here.... When I graduated, I was raised in rank to that of HA 2/c .... It's one step that would take a year in peace time." As his main duty this first day, Walter "...wheeled out about 25 patients 3 blocks to make room for more. I really worked hard." He provides no further details and I imagine him at an intersection with a gurney waiting for the light to change.

As usual a portion of his letter is about the ranch - the premium quality of the baby chicks Myrtle ordered, and whether they will be worth the higher price. He touches on brother Byron's never-ending struggle with his vehicles, and the futile, ongoing battle to prevent the coyotes from killing the new lambs. Walter's brother David remembers that while Walter was gone, coyotes killed twenty-one lambs in twenty-one days – a ruinous number out of a flock of less than a hundred ewes.

Although he is going to Bremerton, Walter is not satisfied. "I was disappointed in my grades because I missed the honor roll by 0.6 of a point." A chronology of Walter's comments about corpsman's school reveals how much he has changed and how quickly.
January 21 – "I am quite sure I won't get in." (Prior to taking the test, Walter is pessimistic.)

January 30 – "Boy oh boy I made it!" (Walter is excited to be accepted into corpsman's school.)

February 9 – "Still can't believe it." (The news is too good; something could go wrong.)

February 12 – "Don't know if I can do it, but I'll try." (Doubts he can name 206 bones in body.)

February 26 – "I'll try to be in first 25 in class." (On March 19 he graduated 37 out of 160.)

March 16 – "I got a 98." (Walter's score on the nursing portion. Final average 94.6.)

March 20 – "Boy oh boy I made Bremerton!" (Walter's hard work has paid off.)

Two months ago, Walter had never seen the ocean, a zoo or even a moderately large city. Now he has seen both ocean and zoo and become accustomed to life on a Navy base in the middle of a city of over 200,000 souls. Two months ago, he doubted he could pass an entrance exam for corpsman school and feared that if he got into the school, he would not be able to grasp the material.

Despite his worries, or perhaps because of them, Walter worked. He studied, he practiced, he took notes. Walter reduced difficult problems to their individual parts, then memorized the solutions. He volunteered for extra duties, accepted correction, and always showed respect. Myrtle had trained him well. Seventy or so years later, he revealed why his scores were higher than some better educated men. "I cheated! I noticed that the bold-faced material in the handouts was always on the tests, so I just memorized that."

On Monday, March 23, Walter is ready to leave San Diego. "Dear Folks, I can hardly believe it's true but tomorrow I'll be on the way up north…. I'll always remember the first time I saw the ocean." With time hanging heavy, Walter has time for nostalgia and complaints. "Gee how I'd like to get some hot, fresh, home-baked bread…. Here they have baker's bread. The butter is terrible, and I haven't had a decent drink of milk since I came here."

In his next sentence Walter uses 'terrible' to describe a very different event. "We had a terrible thing happen here. I don't remember whether or not I told you about it or not." (Whack! Ouch! The specter of Miss Fink, Walter's senior year English teacher, materializes and strikes him sharply on the wrist with her sharp-edged ectoplasmic ruler. "That is a double negative, Mr. Dodd, I'll see you after school.")

The 'terrible thing' he refers to is a bit of horseplay gone amiss. The boys decided that two students, those with the highest and lowest test scores, should be thrown into the 'fish pond,' a shallow, decorative pond adjacent to the mess hall. Tempers became inflamed and someone encouraged someone else to occupy a space already filled by a large plate glass window. The destruction of government property in wartime prompted the words 'court martial,' and the entire company, including Walter, was mustered, although as he notes in his letter, "Neil, Fullerton and I were in the shower." Protestations of innocence were universal, and the men dismissed. Minutes later, the men were re-mustered and encouraged to double-time through a series of brisk maneuvers for about an hour until recruit Grosdidier did everyone a favor by collapsing from exhaustion. The next day, once the men's free will donations for the window reached $25, the matter was deemed closed.

He describes his last day in San Diego, which he spends in the base hospital. "I am in the surgery ward no. 2. That is where all hernia and appendix cases come, 6-15 a day. I would hate to be a patient here. Three nurses for 50 patients & about 4 regular corpsmen but most of them are so lazy they aren't worth their salt. Some of these rated men, 3rd class pharmacists, don't know anything more about nursing than I do. Funny having them ask us how to do things."

After watching a couple operations Walter apparently roams the hospital a bit. "I went over to the psychopathic ward (nut house) and looked them over. The ones in the separate cells sort of scare me, they look so much like apes. Their eyes are terrible." Back in February, when he first visited the zoo, Walter was impressed by the gorilla - "Boy could he sit back and stare."

The rest of his letter trails off with details about class schedules, questions as to the proper clothing for the journey to Bremerton, and comments on men he will miss when they go to their separate assignments. At least he and Neil will be together, as they have been ever since they left Missoula. "Well I think I'll go to sleep perhaps I won't have such a good rest for a couple nights. Good night, Walter – address in question at present – U.S. Naval Hospital Staff, San Diego Calif"

PART 3 – BREMERTON – 104 LETTERS,
MARCH 24, 1942 – FEBRUARY 19, 1943

W alter's letter of March 27 is full of wonder. "Well I am here after two days and nights on the way.... I certainly like it here although they haven't assigned me any duties yet. Neil and I rode together and now we are in the same room. It's swell, second floor, lots of light, even a table & chair.... This morning I woke and heard the robins. Gee that was swell. Everything is more like home. Down there was almost like going to a different country."

In addition to active-duty personnel and their families, the Bremerton Naval Hospital cares for veterans and, on occasion, civilians working at the base. They treat every imaginable injury and malady, deliver babies, and care for drunks. Walter has hardly seen anything yet, but he is hopeful.

Compared to "Dago", the Bremerton hospital is much superior, "... so clean looking and we serve ourselves even milk, good milk.... Here the Chief Petty Officers eat with the regular corpsmen, something they would never think of doing down there."

The drive from the train depot to the ferry terminal spooked him a bit. "...the streets seemed narrow and rather dark from the tall buildings... boy they sure drive fast and close. It wouldn't be fun to drive here." The scenery made up for the drive. "It's possible we will be stationed here for 3 or 4 months. I'd like to make it permanent. You can't imagine how nice it was to see pine and fir again."

He fills almost a page with a dozen little details about his room, and wonders when he will be granted liberty so he can see his uncle's dairy, Marymoor Farms. "What's the weather like there now? Here the jonquils are in bloom and the lilacs are leaving.... It will be fun watching spring come again.... Well it's time for class. I'll write again soon. Perhaps we'll be very busy again. Hope everything is O.K. & you're all well. Love Walter US Naval Hospital, Bremerton, Washington. H.C.Q. P.S. 'H.C.Q.' stands for Hospital Corpsmen's Quarters and that's my address I guess."

On April 2 Walter begins a five day stretch of daily letters home, totaling 12 pages. During the month of April, his 14 letters home will fill 43 hand written pages. Based on his comments, he likely writes just as many to others - aunts and uncles, cousins, and friends.

April 2, "Dear folks, I'm very tired tonight (4:30). This makes three days in ward F which is contagion. We have Scarlet fever, mumps, and measles, both kinds. I don't especially care for it because we have to fool around with the gowns, masks and wash our hands in antiseptic water every time we turn around. It's sort of dangerous because the regular doctor has the mumps now. We have Pop Calhoun, an old Spanish American War Vet, in for a build-up. He's not especially sick now although yesterday noon he got sick to his stomach and when he started to vomit and run off at the bowels, they put me in as special watch.... It makes a very long day. I used to sympathize with the nurses, now I can sympathize with myself." Some corpsmen might gripe but Walter has kept his sense of humor. He has no complaints about the nurses he works for and I suspect Myrtle has taught him to automatically show respect to women.

Walter's exhaustion is not helped by the schedule. "Here we put in one day of from 6:30 to 2:30 & then an hour of class and the next day from 8 A.M. to 9 P.M. It makes a very long day." The afternoon classes are lectures and "...so far they haven't amounted to much."

He seldom speaks with Neil, who is on a different shift. The food here is good, better than in San Diego. Walter is planning to trade shifts with another corpsman so that on April 12 he can visit his relatives at

Marymoor farms. He closes with a short, paragraph about events back home, and puts the letter in the mail.

In another letter the next day, Walter describes the confusion that ensued **after** he had mailed his April 2 letter. After Walter got off shift, Neil received a letter from his parents saying that Walter's parents were coming to see Walter "over the week end." In addition, Lloyd, Walter's uncle, telegraphed to advise that "they", presumably Walter's parents, were coming to visit "Saturday." Walter was upset - "It really bothered me to think you came without telling me." - but what could he do? Almost immediately, the situation degenerated into slapstick worthy of Laurel and Hardy. Walter showed the telegram to the captain who granted him a special week end liberty. Then Walter realized that neither the letter nor the telegram mentioned a specific week end, and had the captain cancel the liberty. Next, Neil hurried in with news that Walter's folks were in Bremerton. Somehow, Walter got his liberty restored and even extended to a second day.

When Walter and Neil arrived at the Bremerton YMCA where they were supposed to meet Walter's parents, they met instead Myrtle's sister, Ruby, and her husband John. John had wheedled a hotel room, supposedly an impossible task. Walter had always been especially close to aunt Ruby, and they all visited happily till almost midnight, so in the end, all was well.

April 4, 1942, "Well I'll send my Easter greetings although you won't receive them on time…. I've three letters piled up from home, one from Mrs. Davis and one from Wallace." Although it is less than 500 miles from Missoula to Seattle, letters can take up to fourteen days to make the trip, about the same as in San Diego which is over twice the distance.

"Right now I'm on my ward (F, contagion) treating measles, mumps and chicken pox." Walter is taking an extra shift so another corpsman can go see his folks. Walter refused to accept pay for this, and later in the letter mentions to his folks that he does not need extra cash and plans to send money home.

Walter explains his plan to visit Marymoor farm, the Redmond dairy farm operated by Pop's brothers, Ralph, and Dean Dodd. Such a visit would start with a ferry ride from the Bremerton Naval Base, located on the southern tip of the Kitsap Peninsula, across the Puget Sound to the Seattle terminal. The drive from terminal to farm would be about 15 miles. Walter has wanted to see the farm for some time, and now telephones the farm, where he reaches Lloyd Dodd, another one of Pop's seven brothers. Lloyd tells Walter to let them know when he is coming and promises to pick him up at the dock. A round trip ferry ticket is $.95, so once Walter earns a weekend liberty, he will be all set.

The letter skips over the usual weather and health reports, so apparently spring has sprung, and folks must be fine. After just one week in Bremerton, he makes his first complaint about the food. "Boy I'd like to taste some warm buns & warm bread again. We couldn't ask for better food, they buy the best & expensive stuff but it's still not home cooked."

Walter disapproves of one the favorite pastimes of sailors. "Gee I get tired of watching the fellows gamble. All the time day & night there's a nickel poker, crap, or just some other card game. It costs some of them quite a bit of money. Some of those southerners sound funny throwing dice. They make more noise than a crowd at a prize fight." He can also be cynical and quick to judge. "Maybe Mordy (a relative) has 'struck it rich.' It won't do them any good though. He wouldn't be anyone to work with I don't believe although there might be money in it. He'll probably spend it on liquor what she doesn't."

Walter tries to apply some of his new medical knowledge to the sheep. "I believe no. 74 had better be discarded; she's no good. Perhaps you'll have to start an isolation ward for those sick lambs. It may be contagious. Have any of the sheep still got worms?

"I've been reading the orders of the hospital…better than 100 pages. We are supposed to know all that, and in case of infractions, ignorance is no excuse. I have broken some of the rules but haven't been called on them…. Someone said you can do anything in the Navy if you can get away with it. I'd rather not crowd my luck too far."

"April 5, Dear Folks, Well I'm planning on your visit…. I will be able to get my liberty especially if you send a telegram saying you're arriving at a certain time. Chief Rickard knows you are coming and said he would see when I asked him for weekend liberty." Walter is taking no chances. The telegram should prevent a repetition of last week's non-visit.

Walter has a request. "Mother look on my graduation certificate...I will have to have the date to know when I might go up for my next test. My guess would be March 22." The actual date is March 19, and though Walter left San Diego only ten days ago, he no longer remembers the date of his graduation from corpsman's school. He is truly living in the now.

"Neil wants to go on liberty tomorrow night and especially that I come along. It doesn't seem like liberty unless we're together. This is a pretty nice group of fellows working here – still can't get away from the Texans though.... Chief Richard is going to get special pay for us... because we were in transit.... I guess I'll give the money to you – I don't want to carry it. This visit to the farm will save me writing 3 or 4 letters.... I guess that will be all for tonight, but I'll be seeing you – Love Walter."

"April 6, Dearest Folks, I took D.' s place Saturday afternoon so that he could go home.... I sort of liked the duty over the week end as I wouldn't have gone out and there was practically no work to do.... We have more soldiers & Marines for patients than sailors. Perhaps that's because they lead a rougher life.... Lots of fellows I have met from Mont. 4 right around me in the barracks." Walter spends a paragraph discussing the ranch before stopping in frustration. "A fellow's bothering me – a blowhard.... Guess I'll go & iron. Love to all, Walter".

April 8 - "I'll try to finish that letter I was writing the other night. That fellow gets my goat. He keeps gloating over the fact that a couple of 15-year-old girls are competing in writing love letters to him. He encourages it." All his life Walter was deeply offended by lies and had no time for blowhards.

"I rated liberty tonight my third so far, but I washed and wrote a letter to Mrs. Davis. She sent me an Easter card and sent me a writing portfolio.... Stamps, envelopes and some post cards were included." Violet Davis is Myrtle's first cousin, and even though she and Myrtle have never met in person they have corresponded for years. Walter will write to Mrs. Davis throughout his service.

He continues, "I don't mind, in fact I sort of like ward work other than the cleaning. The patients always hate the place & hope for the day of departure but 3 or four have said when the day came, they weren't so anxious to go. **That guy came around, but I got rid of him!**" The emphasis is Walter's, and it is clear he is referring to the blowhard.

Walter tells more about his job's do's and don'ts. Put simply, do everything a nurse or doctor requests, and don't improvise. Follow the rules. If an aid breaks a thermometer, he loses his next liberty. He notes that two aids, who were caught making up a patient's TPR record, (temperature, pulse, and respiration) are in serious trouble. Walter does his job and gets along fine with the nurses, doctors, and patients – probably everyone with the exception of the 'blowhard.' Most of the patients know his name and some think he's about 19 even though he will turn 24 in October.

Besides loud-mouthed braggarts, a couple other things bother him. "My but there has been a lot of candy on the ward. It doesn't seem right for them to eat that way. They send down for more from the canteen." Of more consequence, some of the patients get little or no mail. "The other day I stopped my work to read my mail & one of the patients came by & said he hadn't received any since he hit port and was in the hospital. Some folks don't seem to realize what a letter does for a patient." Walter certainly doesn't want for mail himself, and he sympathizes with others who are less fortunate.

On April 14, almost a week since he last wrote, Walter cranks out a six-page letter. He has finally made it to Marymoor. There he met Pop's brothers and their families. He lists fifteen adults by name.

Marymoor is a big operation with 200 Guernsey cows, and Walter is impressed. "It's a swell place – a great many buildings. There are two large barns ... that they can use for hay storage & dry stock. They have chicken house room for 10,000 Bill says.... You ought to see all the machinery they have, 2 tractors, thrashing machine, 4 trucks.... Their system of milking is swell & they have a huge plant for taking care of the milk." He is not entirely overawed. "I didn't think much of their sheep. Small and rather poor for the good pasture.... You know they can get $25 for a scrub buck here not as large or nice as ours. Their herd is rather rough now ... but they are nice cows."

Even on the farm, the war is a constant presence. "They have been so seriously warned about invasion that they each have a rifle & plenty of ammunition." While Walter was there, "A couple of girls came out... the girls offered to bring me back. Seems strange how a uniform affects girls. They'd never have noticed me otherwise."

April 16 - "We got five new corpsmen on our ward. Four of the old ones shipped out. Miss Walters made me senior corpsman second in command. That means I must do the charting, reports, and give medication. I'm awful tired. I rate liberty tonight but even if it were good weather, I wouldn't go. I wish I could get the ambition.... I will probably be here for 3 more weeks." Because I know he will remain in Bremerton well into 1943, I am puzzled by his last comment, and can only put it down to Walter's unfamiliarity with the wild rumors that permeate the Navy. With time, he will learn not to give credence to any scuttlebutt until he sees the orders in writing.

He continues, "Of course it would be awful nice to see you, but you can best tell how & when or if you will come. I don't know how I could get away from the hospital very far.... Maybe if you came, I could get special liberty, but that's entirely up to the captain... Love Walter."

Walter's April 18, letter causes me to wonder if he is insecure, or just modest. Describing some family pictures he writes, "If I'd pulled in my ears or perhaps just faded out the pictures would have been swell." Later, after a senior corpsman gives Walter some notes to help him study for a new rating, Walter writes, "Everyone is so nice to me. I sometimes wonder why. I never seem to do much for others." Does he realize this statement is patently false? Walter has spent the last two months preparing for a job whose sole purpose is taking care of others.

In his personal relationships Walter has more than once worked shifts for other corpsmen. He has made small no interest loans to fellow recruits who were a little short. He has done his share and more, never sluffed off and been a good friend.

So why would he feel he is undeserving? At the beginning Walter was insecure and very pessimistic about his chances of becoming a corpsman. Since then he has competed successfully against better educated, more experienced men and through hard work, proved himself over and over. I see no reason for low self-esteem, so what is going on?

When I was a child, Walter taught me that pride was a particularly corrosive sin. I'm sure it was the same with him, and when he said, "Don't blow your own horn. Don't get too big for your britches. Be careful not to break your arm patting yourself on the back." I'm sure he was just repeating what Myrtle told him as a boy. Now, in the Navy, where braggarts and blowhards abound, Walter remains a modest person. As he gains knowledge and develops skills, it is to be hoped he can learn to accept praise without guilt.

News has just come in about Doolittle's raid, and Pop Calhoun, the Spanish American War Vet, is still on Ward F. As Walter writes, "He is very excited about the bombing of Tokyo. He figures the Axis are about thru. I wish that he were right but I'm sure they are far from done. It will take more effort & sacrifice than we've given so far to win." Walter is in a reflective mood. "You know Ward F seems like the closest thing to home for me. The first thing I did when I returned Monday was to hurry over. I notice that other corpsmen do the same thing. When on liberty they are apt to go by the ward or to stop in there on their days of standby."

Walter still has his gentle, self-deprecating sense of humor. "Sunday 19, I'm sitting at the nurses desk acting big. Well I wasn't called last night & got the full amount of sleep. Everything seems quiet at present. It's a relief... Love to all, Walter."

April 22 – "No chance of getting a permanent place here. Even the Drs & nurses change fast. Now they have changed our ward. It was contagion. Now we have convalescence. One bed patient and the rest go on liberty every other night.... It's not very nice now, we have to look for work." Some patients are happy to be discharged, but there are others. "Another patient is leaving also. I'm glad... because he'd have stayed another month, just a lazy baby from Texas. He never did anything in his life." This is Walter's second disparagement of Texans as a group. It is a lifelong bias. Ten years later, in one of life's perfect ironies, Walter marries a Texas country girl – my mother.

With less to do, Walter starts taking more liberty, and sometimes walks back through the shipyard among the immense ships where he notices that many of the workers are women. Much of his free time is spent writing letters. "Gee I've got about all the correspondence I want. It takes plenty of time … seems like I get a letter every other day now."

Walter has observed his first autopsy. "He died from a ruptured appendix. I hear it was ruptured some time before he was removed from his ship. He lived a long time. The Drs gave him practically no chance long before he died although they really worked for him. One said he lasted too long – he just suffered useless pain…. He stunk something terrible. He was rotten and full of puss in his abdomen. The Lt. Junior grade was very nervous." From his description, one might expect Walter to be averse to watching future operations, but quite the opposite. "I'll go next time I have a chance. I'd like to see a heart case, appendectomy or something major."

Walter's April 25 letter is inconsequential, entertaining and six pages long. First, he devotes almost an entire page to an ongoing, two-day argument among the corpsmen about the definition of idiosyncrasies. Walter offers two spellings, both incorrect, but finally settles on a meaning: "A peculiarity of a person in which he acts differently under similar circumstances than the average."

A second page chronicles the corpsmen's research and speculation into the geographical origin, age, and marital status of Miss Walters, the head nurse. Their conclusions? She is from Sitka, Alaska, about 23 years old, and divorced. They have no hard evidence for any of these 'facts' and rely instead on "scuttlebutt".

Finally, after mentioning that he plans to go to church the next day, Walter reveals that the canteen on the ground floor sells beer. "And boy do they do the business. It's the first ship's store that most fellows have heard of that sells alcohol. It's a Marine canteen." This is apparently explanation enough.

It is clear that Walter is quite comfortable when he writes, "You know I believe I'm getting lazy. I sort of enjoy setting around here now, at first it bothered me something terrible. Here I'm sitting at the nurses desk acting like I owned the place."

"Bremerton, Wash, April 27, I spent Sunday from 2:00 to 9:00 P.M. copying my course. I got all but one assignment copied."

Walter refers to 'copying courses' many times but never explains what he means. A 'course' consists of a sheet of printed questions on a particular medical topic. There appear to be no textbooks, so the medical information must come from lectures and perhaps handouts. A student is expected to take good notes.

Each man completes a course by filling in the answers based on his notes. Each course can run for several pages. Courses are turned in, graded, and returned to be used as study guides for the tests that will eventually follow. The highest possible grade is 4.0 and Walter typically scores 3.7 to 3.9.

'Copying' a course happens when Jones fills out a course, submits it, gets it back, and allows Smith to copy it for a fee. Some might call this cheating but the budding corpsmen at Bremerton call it normal. The going rate to copy a course is $3 or $4. I believe Walter does most, and perhaps all, of his own work.

The ward nurse, Miss Walters, has been replaced by… "Rathenhafer, a very jolly, attractive young lady. Hair as black as it comes & good looking…. The main occupation of the patients & corpsmen is to keep her entertained." It seems that Walter is also under her spell. "Today Rathy complimented me on hiding a bottle before the chief nurse realized what I had. It was vinegar to wash the windows with."

Walter is particularly impressed by Lt. Duncan, one of the doctors. "Boy he's a swell fellow, rather young, mild but very highly respected. He is quite widely known as a surgeon up & down the coast. He has me come in his office & help with his reports, always calls me by name."

Walter's best friend Neil has applied for regular duty in surgery, a position that would likely last at least six months. Walter does not particularly want to stay in Bremerton, in fact he has become bored. "Today they put a notice up on the board … announcing a test for HA 1/c but we have to be in the service for 8 months before we may take it…. You know I'm getting so I wouldn't mind going to sea. I'd advance faster, I hear."

Walter closes, saying he hopes his folks can visit him in the next few weeks and asking them -twice - to please bring his typewriter if they do. Considering his output of letters, the multiple daily reports he must submit, and the pages of study notes he generates, a typewriter would be welcome.

On April 30, two days later, Walter writes again. He will be assigned effective May 1 to the dispensary, located in another part of the Navy yard. Workers there apparently get frequent liberty, and he encourages his parents not to change their plans to visit.

Initially, Walter is not displeased by the reassignment. "Well I'm through with another job – rather glad too. Changing nurses so often in the last few days made it very hard." Of course, a transfer requires lots of signatures, but by the time he is finished, Walter understands the drill. "Did we have a time getting our check out cards signed. We had to run down the officers and didn't know who to look for or where they were at. We caught some in the halls & some in offices & got the yeomen of some to sign. I didn't get one signature, but they took the card, so I guess it's O.K. ... We were from 1500 till 1730 getting about seven signatures."

Walter does harbor some regrets about the sudden move. "Our ward was just getting interesting again. We were getting surgical patients. We got two today & one more scheduled day after tomorrow. I had to keep track of the blood pressure, pulse, and respiration for the first two hours, checked them every 15 minutes on the two patients.... I have the ward prepared for inspection but won't be there."

He will be working with 'Rathy' again, though he does not refer to her by name. "One of the nurses that was on for a while on my ward is going down there. She'll be the only nurse there. She'd better be there too – she's got my handbook; boy are they scarce & in demand – I've been offered twice the price for it."

Walter tells his folks he should be able to get the liberty he has planned and urges them to go ahead with their trip the following week. He will telegraph Myrtle's brother if they need to cancel. "Guess I'll close.

Sorry to hear you have a cold. Last night I had a stopped up head but OK now. Wishing you lots of health & love, Walter"

Walter occasionally mentions eighteen-year-old Byron, but usually only to remind him of some ranch work that needs to be done, to chide him about missing a shot at a coyote with their rifle, or to comment on the ongoing problems with Byron's 'wreck' which seems always on the verge of a breakdown.

In the first four months of letters, Walter's father is conspicuous by his absence. Albert is only 54, but perhaps he never completely recovered from the loss of an eye in a winter logging accident years before. My picture of Pop in 1952 cannot explain who he was in 1942, but I can say with assurance that Myrtle absolutely dominated their relationship during my years on the ranch. David confirms my impression, and it is clear that her influence on Walter was very strong.

Sometime in the first part of May, Pop and Myrtle drove to Seattle and visited Walter. There is no record of the date, but on May 14, when Walter writes again, he tells us, "I received your letter today, I've been looking for it. Funny but I haven't written any since 'the visit.' I guess I owe everyone one now. I am dumb and guess I look the part.... Mr. Rickard gave me a 48.' I took it to mean a 48-hour liberty. It does but it starts at 0800 Sat & is terminated 0800 Mon. So I was 3 hours overleave. I went right to work and when Mr. Rickard asked me what the trouble was, I told him I didn't know there was any. Anyway he started laughing and told me he would fix it up. I wasn't even restricted but I've certainly taken ribbing. Several said they have thought of pulling that story but didn't have the courage.... You know when I started working on my course studying, the chiefs didn't want me to stop to do any errands. They certainly are nice.... We didn't get a chance to visit alone very much but it certainly was swell while it lasted.

"May 17, Dear Folks, I received your letter yesterday and since today is so quiet I'll answer it now." Myrtle's last two letters arrived on the 14th and 16th of May, confirming that she too is a prolific correspondent. Perhaps this is an inherited trait?

"This has been a bad week, I got in late… gone to chow on the wrong shift & seems everything has been bad. DeVore, who came down from the hospital with us, was overleave a week ago, just overslept & served his one-week restrictions. Then Fri. night went home, he's married, & overslept again. This time he has a two-week restriction." This is our introduction to Lloyd DeVore, a fellow corpsman, and a likeable rascal. DeVore will appear in many of Walter's letters.

"Another fellow who was restricted went out anyway…. He was sent up for a summary court marital… and not allowed to go up for his new rate…. I believe I'll go up to the dentist and have him check my teeth. I seem to have a sharp edge on one. DeVore is having them work on his. They seem to be doing a good job.

"The other day there was a soldier fell 3 stories & they called for this ambulance. The driver took it outside the gates contrary to regulations & is waiting to see what will happen. The poor fellow might have died before they could have gotten a civilian driver to take him over." Walter never clarifies this incident but apparently some Navy rule has been broken and the driver may be punished regardless of mitigating circumstances.

Walter's life has settled into a routine at Bremerton and his letters reflect that. Typically, he covers his daily activities and his health. He reports on letters he has written and those he needs to write. With nine uncles, three aunts, and a plethora of cousins, keeping up is quite a task. Walter no doubt responds to their latest joys and afflictions, but his life right now belongs to the Navy.

"May 18, … I got the money order, the pictures which I'll mail, and my iron fixed. A fellow borrowed it & broke the handle right down close to the iron. So I took it up town to be welded. afraid it would cost more than the iron was worth… a fellow at a battery service fixed it -swell – for – 25 cents.

"You know some of the passages in the Bible raise some questions. Does it sound to you like it means you are not supposed to acquire property or wealth? I can see no reason for that if honestly made & you don't renounce everything else for that aim…. You don't happen to know how much money I have sent home do you? ...Be sure & tell me if the money order comes thru…. Love Walter"

May 23, "Last night Neil and I went ashore and saw a movie…. They also put a very solemn sermon in it about liquor…. The Chiefs were talking the other day & said there was less drunkenness & fights now than in the 'good old days. I certainly saw one example of too much the other night. That poor sap was out and very sick. I went to sleep before they got through treating him – wasn't very interested although I guess I should know how."

Walter is impressed by his first jeep ride. "They ride nicer than our ambulance… Boy I'd like to have one to play around with."

He also shows some dark medical humor. "Those yard birds must think we're a bloodthirsty outfit when we greet them 'How badly are you bleeding?' and 'O good, another victim.' We do it especially to patients that we know. Guess it's about my turn to do a suture job. Business is rather brisk tonight."

For a second time, either in response to one of Myrtle's letters, or due to contact with some Jehovah's Witnesses, Walter raises a biblical question. "St. Mathew and St. Luke seem to be about the same don't they. How do you explain – easier may a camel pass thru the eye of a needle than for a rich man reach the kingdom of heaven & later the verse saying more will be given to those who have & those that haven't even the little they have will be taken away?" Walter resolves to read further.

In his personal life Walter's attitude toward money can best be described as frugal. "This week has been nice, … looking forward to nothing but pay day as all good sailors do. Don't know why though I've about $7 left. One fellow certainly gets my goat. We never get too mad at him but often disgusted. He's always begging but quite generous immediately after pay day. Always eats at the canteen until his money is gone. Has no soap of his own and all sorts of little things. Won't be sorry to see the last of him. Lights out. Goodnight, Walter."

May 27 - Its Wednesday and cases are coming in fast. Walter interrupts his letter to dress two lacerations and half a page later is hit by "two sprains, a fractured fibula, and innumerable contusions and lacerations.... It's quitting time ... Love to all, Walter."

On Friday, May 29, a lot of the men have been asking Walter for loans. He tries to write but is too busy. One man staggers in with a lacerated thumb, which seems to signal a rush of others. He manages another half page before four show up at once. "Guess I'll sign off, too many interruptions."

June 2, and Walter is in good spirits. He has typed forty pages of the course for the PM3c exam and is over half done.

Walter offers no explanation when he writes "... all week ends have been canceled & we had to sign an order that we wouldn't leave the immediate vicinity of Bremerton." Japanese submarines were active off the Pacific coast that June, and later in the month a Japanese sub bombarded Fort Stevens at the mouth of the Columbia River. The shells did little damage, but increased fears that a more serious attack might be imminent.

As Walter writes, everyone on the Base is on edge and emotions are out of control. The Chiefs, who a few weeks ago had time to swap lies in daily bull sessions, are now short tempered and curt as they rush to inventory supplies and struggle to place orders. Outside on the dock the Seattle ferries, which were supposed to be suspended, continue to run. Walter remains focused on the pharmacist course he is typing. He thinks he could sell a finished copy for about $10.

Besides testing for his next rating, (HA1C), Walter hopes to make a visit home before being deployed. "I've been thinking, one of the nicest things I would like to do would be to set posts over on the Grant Creek side & eat a lunch & lots of cold milk. Just to be alone for a whole day & watch the traffic on the road but be no part of it." Seldom does he let his guard down so honestly and having done so, he is quick to close. "I'd appreciate some sunshine – 2 or 3 full days of it. All we have is a few minutes now and then. Love to all, Walter".

On Saturday, June 6, he notes, "I average one letter a day it seems. Lots of work for Uncle Sam keeping me informed of the welfare of my relatives." He admits to doing as little as possible. "I'm getting very lazy.

165 lbs. of adipose tissue. The nurse was talking to Chief Kersey today as if she wanted Knad to take my place. She said he could sit just as well as I could." Walter studies, but otherwise he is just marking time.

As he waits, he writes a quick note to David. "I'm sorry I haven't written …Mom tells me you had some radishes… Do the airplanes fly around there much?... It is almost bed time. Goodnight."

By June 8, Walter has indeed been shanghaied. Miss Rathenhafer has him spending two hours a day in the Emergency Care Center. Already he has "… been on an ambulance call, stood watch on an epileptic case, sutured a lacerated hand, & redressed several older & some new wounds."

Walter is worried about DeVore. "I'm thinking DeVore is going to have marital troubles. His wife likes him, and he seems to love her a great deal, but he just gets drunk whenever he's with her…. Guess I'll close for tonight."

Almost all of Walter's writing now happens while he is supposedly on duty, and on June 10, he picks up where he left off. Liberty is still restricted, and Walter misses the hot dry Montana summers. "Haying already! You couldn't here. It's really rained here the past few days." After the usual family gossip, he notes, "Tonight I bandaged up a fellow's finger, Smith, F.O., as I remember, whose breath smelled of whiskey so badly it nearly made me sick. I asked the Dr. if we were supposed to report it. This one said guess we wouldn't try to do any policing." He then describes a janitor. "A Filipino. He's going to re-enter the Navy soon. Quite a fellow 5' 2" & weighs 115 lbs. He's very strong. He says he can press 150 lbs. over his head."

Friday, June 12, he writes, "The weather was swell today. Sun all day but news not so good. Lexington down and Jap landings in the Aleutian Islands." The Lexington sank over a month before, but the Alaska news is almost current. Walter and the other corpsmen are restless – they expect to be transferred, but not knowing the where or when is unsettling.

June 14 - "Saturday was a swell day. Neil and I went to a movie, ate a sandwich & strawberry shortcake with soft ice cream. That was real ice cream…. We started out and walked till 10 PM. Certainly was nice to get out in the country.

"I am wishing you congratulations, best wishes, or whatever is due you, Pop, upon this Father's Day.... Yesterday I stenciled a red cross on innumerable helmets. I wonder what good they would do against a Jap....

"June 16... Well today Lana Turner came thru the yard & helped pep up the workers. We could see the platform from our step but only a few went down to see her. My but it sounds bad the way they say there will be no more rubber. Hope your tires will last 2 ½ years. Byron won't be able to drive at that rate. Are you going to collect all of the old tires from around the place?" Walter worries about scarcity and prices, but never mentions gas rationing. Farmers were receiving extra gas because their work was deemed critical to the war effort.

Walter describes a sailor who "... came in & had a Bogens run on him. He has a 2.0 test. Quite high." Walter is referring to a breath test for blood alcohol level developed by Dr. Emil Bogen in 1927. As he mentioned in his June 10 letter, Walter is almost nauseated by the stink coming off a drunk.

His short note has become two pages. "The Japs are getting a little now. I believe the papers play up small victories though. Probably we're losing more than they are in ships. Sounds as if our airplanes are much better or perhaps the pilots are largely responsible for that.... My but there was a crowd to see Turner today. I heard anyone could kiss her who put $25,000 into bonds.... Many were disappointed. They lined up along the sidewalk in town, but she came directly into the yard in a chartered boat or something .... Guess I'll sign off Walter."

June 22, - Walter has had an adventure and for almost three pages the Navy is just an inconvenience and the war is the last thing on his mind. "Dear Family, Well I did it. Out to Alvin and Ruth's and back again. I didn't know that I could go until 20 minutes before I left. Mr. Rickard told me definitely that I couldn't go.... One hour before C. was to go on his week end, the captain caught him asleep & cancelled his liberty.... I hurried up, & Rickard granted it to me. Boy things went fine. Started at 12 and arrived about 4:30."

Pop's brother Alvin and his wife Ruth lived near the mountain hamlet of Whitehorse, eighty miles NW of Seattle. From the Seattle ferry terminal, Walter made his way to the bus stop and there, after just a 10 minute wait, caught a thru bus to Arlington for $1.16. Whitehorse, twenty-five miles east of Arlington, sat at the end of a mostly gravel road, and had limited bus service, so Walter decided to hitch-hike. The fourth car took him to within ¼ mile of Alvin's.

"Certainly surprised them…. I had a swell time. She had a cake & Sunday some fresh strawberry shortcake. Boy that was swell – much better than restaurant stuff." After reporting on the family's health and the crops, he writes "Alvin has a nice place. All land like in 'the bottom.' Much of it covered with just such brush."

Back in Montana on the family ranch, 'the bottom' was a flat, brushy area south of the house. Butler Creek flowed through the area and supported a wide variety of plant and animal life. The 'bottom' was one of my favorite places and I imagine Walter felt the same. His visit to Alvin's is a brief, nostalgic interlude and Walter is on base by 10:30 pm Sunday.

Back at the hospital he discovers, "A fellow had been killed. A press was stuck & he looked under it & worked something & it came down & crushed his head. He lived for a short while after arriving at the hospital. We had a terrible bloody mess sheets, pillows etc. to clean up." Welcome back to reality, Navy style.

The evening of June 24, besides his folks, Walter writes to a cousin, her friend, and an aunt. He is on duty, but it is an unusually slow night. "Dear Folks, Mr. Rickard is getting all hepped up again about making me a qualified driver… I don't care for it. Too many small errands that need to be done as well as care for the cars. Gus wants me to type him out a course for Pharmacist 3/c. Guess I will but haven't decided whether to accept any money for it. Maybe I'll take $2.50 about half what is usually charged…. Rickard has given the keys of the bag room to me to take care of. That's nothing but it does mean they expect me to start doing something."

Walter has learned to enjoy being idle. He has referred to himself as 'lazy' in several letters, and apparently the nurses sometimes have to prod him to accomplish certain chores. It occurs to me that this may be the first time since he was seven or eight that Walter has some serious free time.

Two days later, June 26th, Walter writes a birthday note to his younger brother. "Happy birthday, David. I'm sorry this won't reach you on your birthday but perhaps you can still eat a piece of cake for me. You are 7 years old now.... I'm sending you a little present.... David I am wishing you a happy year and one full of accomplishments. Your brother, Walter." With seventeen years between them, Walter and David were not playmates. David has confirmed that he followed Walter around the place from one job to another. There is no evidence that Walter saw himself as a mentor, but that is how David remembers it.

On June 30, Walter finishes the month with a six-page letter, his longest since leaving home. "Dear Folks, it's been a beautiful day in Bremerton. Must have hit 75 or 80. Gee but I've been busy.... Mother, of course I don't know when I'll be transferred but most of the fellows think I'll stay until I make 3/c, that will be about 5 more months."

Walter mentions money throughout this letter. "Neil borrowed $5 & so did another fellow. I'll be repaid tomorrow as we were paid today ... I'll have to buy another pair of pants.... Neil's folks are borrowing part of his money. I wouldn't care if you used mine. It would go toward the place, but Neil is saving for marriage & he won't get anything from it.... I'm going to send my check home. Time certainly slips past me – sorry David's present was late. Didn't know what else to get him."

David remembers a present (likely this one) from his big brother. He describes it as a fake fountain pen that, when the cap was removed, released a spring that caused a pin to strike a cap-gun cap which then produced a small explosion. "Caps" came in a paper roll and contained compounds of sulfur, potassium, and antimony. According to David, this rather complicated mechanism lasted only a little longer than it has taken me to explain it.

"July 2, Dear Folks, Almost the fourth and it will be just another working day.... the yard will operate as usual so our customers will come in as usual." Behind this ordinary sentence is some history.

Since Myrtle moved her family to the ranch in 1931, July 4 has been special. Besides a family picnic, most work was set aside for one day. Of course, chores went on as usual. Chickens had to be fed and cows milked, but other work was put on hold. This is likely to be Walter's fourth of July without Myrtle's home cooking, hence the rather morose tone of his first two sentences.

However, Walter is not one to nurse a disappointment, and in the next sentence squeezes some humor out of his loss. "I'm disgusted with you folks. If you would just go ahead and kill those few coyotes & be done with it instead of just making them gun shy you wouldn't have to spend your time up there. Must be you like the job. Guess you just go in for big game." After this dig at brother Byron, Walter reveals "I'm a qualified driver now which means ... the past few days I haven't set down more than 15 min at any time. The big supply building covers an acre ... big enough to get lost in, and they send me up there to find a man – 7 stories & a basement. I've found a couple or 3 pretty nice people to help me ... so that helps." Despite what he has said, Walter is not cut out for idleness.

"You know, I'm getting to like this place more now that I'm getting responsibilities – something to plan & look forward to. Some of the fellows were trying to persuade me to go to dental school. I couldn't see it, besides having to go back to Dago, I wouldn't care for the work." It is hard to believe these words are from the same person who, on January 21, after testing for one of the Navy's schools, wrote: "I'm quite sure I won't make one." Walter expresses no doubts concerning his ability. Instead, he turns down the opportunity to enter a lucrative profession, and probably stay clear of actual combat, because 'I wouldn't care for the work'!

As the evening progresses and more patients arrive, Walter is constantly interrupted. Before stopping for the night he writes, "You know it's nice to be in the medical corps... we're called 'Doc'."

His next letter is written over July 4 and 5. It has been very hot, up to 100F, and heat stroke cases are increasing. "So Byron and Pop are both registered. *(for the draft?)* Too bad. Hope we're thru before B, has to go."

Walter has been driving more lately. "Yesterday took '42Packard ambulance & picked up a fellow with injured foot. Some car. We have a dead man in the next room. Don't know any of the facts.... I inspected the first aid locker today and found 3pt. of alcohol gone. Capt. said to replace it. Seems a ship had access to the locker & perhaps took it.... I feel tired out .... Love to all, Walter".

July 9, Walter is still weak though he has no idea why. He is certainly homesick and perhaps depressed. He writes, "... if this were just a vacation, as it more or less has been, I'd like to end it now." He mentions others who have more tangible problems. Neil's fiancé is undergoing major surgery, and Chief Smith is being duped by a fake spiritualist who claims to speak to a dead relative.

Always he does his job and chief Rickard is pleased with his work. Walter writes, "I have noticed that he *(Rickard)* has always been very accommodating to me. It's certainly swell to get along with folks." Walter is polite and a hard worker, so it is no wonder chiefs and nurses like him.

July 13, when Walter writes again, his outlook has brightened. The why of this improvement appears to be his second visit to Marymoor Farm. He arrived earlier than expected, and at a very opportune time.

"They were busy with thrashing peas & were shorthanded as one boy got hurt & 2 men quit. So Sunday, I drove the mower with a windrow attachment connected. It's a terrible job mowing those things. They ball up all the time. Had lots of trouble getting started."

Judging from that description, one might think Walter was unhappy. Quite the opposite. Walter was driving a tractor, not a team of horses, definitely a big plus for him. Even better, with no training or preparation, he had successfully taken on a 'terrible job,' one so bad that two men had walked off. For the next fifty years he will attack all his problems, emotional or otherwise, by attempting to work them to death.

Walter barely mentions the Navy in this cheerful letter, and it is obvious how much the visit has improved his outlook. "Ralph tried to pay me $5 for my day's work. Said it was worth it, but it was fun for me. Love, Walter."

July 14th and Walter writes for the second time in as many days. The weekend at the farm boosted his spirits and neither the Navy nor the rainy weather bothers him. He has received four letters in the past few days from cousins and aunts, and one from Mrs. Pope.

A letter from Luella Pope was not to be ignored. She was educated 'Back East' and came from money. Her husband, Walter, a professor at the University in Missoula, worked as an attorney for the Milwaukee Railroad after graduating from the University of Chicago Law School and was active in the Montana Democratic Party. The Popes lived three miles down Butler Creek Road from the Dodd ranch and were their closest neighbors. Luella had taken a particular interest in Walter's future and continued to write him during his time in the Navy. She and her husband mentored Walter and though they differed politically, he held them in great regard.

The content of Walter's letter is mostly unremarkable. Two things stand out: First, The Emergency Care Center where Walter works is getting a new typist, and Walter's sole comment is, "I hope they don't get a girl." Although he gets along well enough with the female nurses, Walter sees the presence of a woman around so many young men as disruptive and would prefer to avoid it. Second, after closing the letter with "Love to all, Walter" he feels moved to add "Boy but a week-end out there (Marymoor) puts a new outlook on life."

It seems clear, that given a choice, Walter would not return to his family's hardscrabble existence on Butler Creek. He would prefer to have a place like Marymoor Farm where the ground is flat and fertile, the annual rainfall is 40 not 14 inches, and electricity and running water are available. The question is moot. Walter is in the unrelenting, indifferent grip of Uncle Sam for the duration of the World War.

On Saturday, July 18, just before lights out, Walter starts a letter. His duties are going well and as the lead driver, he does more than just pick up orders. "A couple days ago I went out to speed up some of our jobs & today we started to see results." He ranges freely through the electric shop and the machine shop. "You should see the size of the lathes & other machines in there. The building is so crowded with men, & women, & machines one can hardly get around."

Earlier that afternoon, Walter took the station wagon and two other men, and went to an "…apartment barracks sort of housing project…" and moved a doctor to another similar building 100 yards away. "We

...removed the back seat & moved tables, chairs, bed, clothing, dishes, etc. in 4 trips. Missed chow but each made $1.50.... I hear it's time for lights out, finish tomorrow. Goodnight."

On July 19, he writes, "We have a dumb southerner here by the name of Parker – Crash Parker by the way he drives.... Boy but he abuses a car. Took the paint off an ambulance the other day going under a crane that was 1" too low. Love to All, Walter." I wonder, is Crash Parker from Texas perhaps? Probably not or Walter would have said so. Walter gets along with most of his fellow recruits, but I have yet to read anything in his letters about Texans that could be construed favorably.

Later that day, he writes directly to David. "Dear David, I enjoy your letters very much. You seem to be doing a lot of things herding sheep, stacking hay, and helping Mother.... Every Sunday while we ride down to dinner or sometimes other meals the fellows, led by Neil or BK Smith, start singing hymns. Must sound funny coming out of an ambulance or hearse...Your Brother Walter. P.S. Have you killed any coyotes with your pistols? WD."

Walter's July 22 letter finds him frustrated by little things. He can't locate a paint brush; his uniform needs to be re-sized; the fellows won't leave him alone. Worse, he has struggled and failed to procure a typewriter for the new dispensary. His real problem, though, is another corpsman.

"I stood by for Garrett again last night. He said he'd pay. I know he won't, but I won't stand by until he pays me so perhaps, he won't pester me much more." It is common practice among the corpsmen to stand another man's watch for a few dollars. Some men, like Garrett, promise to pay, and then renege. Walter, who sends money home most paydays, is tired of these deadbeats.

Saturday, July 25, Walter writes with a scrap of pertinent news. Another sailor, with 18 months service, has obtained 15 days leave to visit his family. Walter wonders how much leave *he* might get.

Walter and Neil have both established themselves as competent and trustworthy, and Walter pokes a bit of fun at himself. "I'm beginning to feel important around here now – perhaps too much so. Rickard and a Chief were arguing about where something was, & Rickard asked me. When I told him what was at the place, he said, 'His word is good enough for me' and walked off.... Usually I'm sent along to watch the others. Fun now but it will get old soon, I guess.

"He *(Rickard)* spoke of Neil as an outstanding man. You know almost unassisted he has taken over the laboratory.... There is supposed to be a doctor stationed there but ... the Dr. was transferred, and none has replaced him." Chief Kersey needs an operation and will be gone for a few weeks. "It will certainly be difficult without him... he has been my boss and really I have liked him."

Red Wilson, a young sailor who has been assisting Walter, wanted to practice driving in preparation for the test. "So I let him drive, against the rules of course. When backing away from an iron fence he ripped the bumper off. We didn't tell anyone but went to the machine shop and put it back on. It just broke the 4 bolts that held it. Possibly the wrong persons will never hear about it – I hope.... Guess I'll drive... before letting him do it anymore.

"I turned in my 3/C course today.... I have been aboard a merchant ship, an aircraft carrier, a battleship, and a repair ship now. They all look the same below deck.... I'll write Byron later time to quit now ...love to all, Walter."

The next day, July 26, Walter begins, "Dear Byron, Boy has this been a good day for me. No work, just one errand and the rest of the day has been mine. Just now Mr. Rickard told me ... we would get our test tomorrow. Guess I had better do some cramming." Walter breaks off here and picks up the next morning at the same place. "Mr. Rickard sent in our rating papers without giving us a test. He gave me 3.9 – 4.0 being perfect. So I'll be a HA1/C the first of August." Walter adds a couple other comments that could be seen as bragging – something he seldom does – but knowing Walter and Byron's relationship as sibling competitors (Byron by nature being the more aggressive) Walter's small brags are understandable.

On the 28th, Walter ends July with a newsy, four-page letter. He has questions that, with no context, are meaningless. "Well, was it Dassault's bull in the cellar?" and "Does that mean you folks have to pay Wallace's bills? That would be a dirty trick." Again, I wish Myrtle's letters had been preserved.

He relates one incident that could have been extremely serious. "The Drs. At bld. #467 reported that they could not find the narcotics. I don't know what would have happened had it not been there, probably I'd have had to go before the captain, but I could have taken Wilson because we both checked all of the stations. I am more or less responsible for the supplies. They are locked up and I don't think anyone will bother them, so I don't worry. Love to all, Walter."

In Walter's seven months in the Navy, he has written sixty-nine letters home, and at least that many others to relatives, neighbors, and friends. At the Puget Sound Naval Hospital, he has cared for patients in the wards, staffed the Emergency Care Center at night, and driven the ambulance at all hours. He will work in the lab, pharmacy, and surgery before he moves on.

Walter is studious, passing every test, and doing all he is asked. By now he has earned the approval of the nurses. He is polite, respectful, and never raises a fuss. He doesn't drink or brawl and has learned to return from leave on time. Though he began as the Chiefs' dogsbody, he is now their surrogate. If he occasionally bends a rule or oversteps in order to achieve a desired result, he can be confident Rickard and Kersey have his back. He is without personal arrogance and most of the other hospital corpsmen like him. He is even good for small loans – if the man pays it back – and is happy to trade duty if it allows the other guy to visit his family.

His letters describe his daily activities, movies seen, books read, and any interesting medical incidents. He weighs in on cows and crops, lambs and coyotes, Byron's truck, and any other ranch related item. He provides commentary – good or bad, but seldom indifferent - on relatives. He will be at Bremerton for six more months and most of his letters will follow this pattern.

On August 3, Walter suggests the best time for his parents to visit, advises Byron on his endless vehicle woes, and reports on his Washington relative's gardens. He has finally drawn the line with Garrett, the corpsman whose watch Walter stood just a week ago. "I absolutely refused to stand by for Garrett anymore (& he knew why) so Sat. (pay day) he had to come down here to be paid and he paid me so perhaps I'll stand by for him again when it's not inconvenient for me."

He is taking more frequent liberty and enjoying it. "Week end weather was wonderful, so I went through the aquarium… 11 cents admission." He finds humor even in his gripes. "Darn the Chief - it had to be me again to go down and open up for the fellows to get Cokes. Wasted 1 ½ hrs. and out of the writing mood. No telling what I might have said. Love to all, Walter."

On Saturday, August 8, Walter writes his last letter prior to his folks' upcoming visit. He expects to be granted liberty and plans to reserve two hotel rooms.

He shares a sad story, "I helped take a fellow to the hospital that apparently had a heart attack aboard ship …. He died waiting for the Drs up there to come to the emergency room. It made us so mad at first because they were slow, but I guess they couldn't have helped him. He just couldn't get his breath…. We had to strip him and tie him off and place him in the wicker basket in the morgue."

Much of the letter is about alcohol and drunks. "I was given 2 nearly full pints of alcohol to destroy this morning…. No one watched to see what I did with it except 3 workmen were standing by the sewer with their mouths watering. The whole dispensary knew about it by chow time and DeVore said he thought there would be only 2 men who would have done it, Neil, and I…. You see whiskey is taken from yard employees who try to bring it in and bottles with broken seals are destroyed. The new bottles are saved for medicinal purposes.

"DeVore was drunk last night and raised quite a rumpus here. He got kicked in the belly so hard he couldn't get his breath…. He's bruised & sore all over this day…. I won't write Tues as I expect to see you before my letter would get there. Love, Walter."

Ten days later, the family visit is over, and Walter makes no mention of it. His next letter, on August 18, is short and shows Walter hard at work. "I've been studying tonight & every chance. It's 2200 now. Went to bed 2030 last night & slept sound was very tired.... It's going to be hard to prepare for that real inspection Mon... Rickard wants the boiler room floor painted – possibly our storeroom deck painted etc. ...I must go to bed. Love, Walter."

August 26, "Letter time again & guess I'll write on Gov't stationary, using Gov't ink & time about Gov't events & a Gov't employee." Because he is a sailor, his non-airmail letters do not require postage. He just needs to write 'Free" on the upper right hand corner of the envelope and send it off.

On August 28 Walter rushes an officer's wife, who had gone into labor, to the hospital. "Certainly hard to get thru traffic even with the siren wide open... a half hour later the baby was born."

Though this made him late for the final exam for PhM3c, he arrived in time to finish. Walter feels, "We all owe it to Chief Kersey. He got the forms & collected the data & typed them up. We wouldn't be rated except for him." Now Walter is thinking ahead. "I've got to get busy & learn what I'm supposed to know."

He closes for the night, and the next morning writes for five pages with no mention of home or family. He writes instead about his fellow corpsmen and the chiefs. Little of what he writes is of consequence, but he makes one remarkable statement: "My but I enjoy trusting people. Today I didn't mean to, but I did – left this pen laying on 'my' desk and ran out on an ambulance trip. Munski picked it up and just now brought it up to me." Honest himself, Walter is happy because he can trust those around him. This had not been the case in San Diego.

"Gee this afternoon was terrible." This exclamation precedes a half-page description of a woman who fell down some stairs – her subsequent evacuation by stretcher, the ride to the hospital, the x-rays, and her several broken bones. Walter has dealt with many kinds of injuries, but he still hates to see people, especially women, in pain.

Promotions come quickly in wartime and in just one month he has advanced twice. First, from HA2c (Hospital Assistant Second Class) to HA1c, and now to PhMc3 (Pharmacist Mate third class). He will now receive $72 a month. "Some said it didn't pay to work in the navy" he jokes. Out of gratitude Walter spends $6 on a gift - a Ronson lighter personalized with Kersey's initials. As a Navy Chief, a rank equivalent to sergeant, Kersey sits at the intersection between enlisted men and officers and has influence well beyond his rank. Some say, 'sergeants run the army' and Walter seems to agree.

September 8, Walter gets a chance to work with MacLaine, a PhM1c who is very sharp. Walter also drives the ambulance and works with Kersey in stores. A good word for him is dependable. He goes on a short liberty with DeVore. "Saw a bum movie & had dinner. First time he'd gone out without drinking for a long time."

On September 15, after a short visit by his brother Byron, Walter writes somewhat tersely "I guess Byron can tell you all that happened out here." He then moves on to important stuff.

"Last night DeVore got drunk." Walter doesn't say 'again' but it is implied. "Had quite a time. He can't remember much of anything. Used one of his socks to put a tourniquet on a cigar & put it in the desk drawer & couldn't find it the next morning." It is likely that DeVore would have already been severely disciplined for drunkenness if Walter and the other corpsmen hadn't taken care of him.

Walter's September 19 letter begins with a complaint. "Tonight is duty night for me and before I could get the heading typed a Marine came in for an Xray of his left hand and I was the only one who knew how to run the machine.... Night before last was a terrible one. It started out with half of the watch going to the wrong chow and Dr. Price was on ... so most went on report... that night it was so busy the night corpsman had to get most of us up to help him. At one time he had two bad suture jobs and one woman fainted dead away out on the front step.... Yesterday the fire truck ran into the parked ambulance and mashed a fender and Stull got picked up for speeding.... Stull is permanently grounded and restricted indefinitely." Another patient shows up needing X-rays, and again Walter has to step in because "... they knew nothing about this machine – bum watch eh?"

He closes on a lighter note. "Last night DeVore talked me into going to a show with him as an escort to keep him from getting drunk.... We saw Holiday Inn and … a swell cartoon called Puppetoon. It was very good, a satire on the Germans conquering Holland…. Paid today and will send it along… Love Walter."

September 23 – Turnover among the corpsmen and his own seniority give Walter more duties and less free time. "Boy Bamber pulled a boner – a big shot was in to inspect the yard & people were lined up along the street … & an emergency call came & he pulled out fast & had to come back & pick up the stretcher he forgot. A terrible impression for the people. Did we all ever feel hurt."

Though Walter teases Byron, he apparently respects him for his skills in math and chemistry because he sends along a couple of problems converting alcohol solutions from percent volume to percent weight. Walter is studying for his PhM2c exam and wants all the help he can get.

Saturday, September 26, on his day off, he describes the escalating conflict between the Marine M.P.s and the Navy medical staff around the issue of speeding. "Two corpsmen have been grounded. Several officers and officers' wives. The Marines are going on a warpath…. Now we are always a couple miles under the limit – 12 in the main drag and 20 out on the road (inside the yard.) … Everybody seems to be getting a kick out of it."

Walter has solved his math problem without Byron's help and is moving forward. "I typed 18 lessons in two nights about 25 sheets … they have an old typewriter, but I like it."

DeVore is overleave but fudged the paperwork. "Believe he put it over that time. Rickard has told him the next time is the Brig. That's 5 times for him." Walter doesn't directly criticize DeVore and I wonder why.

"I was put on an extra ECC watch the other night to hold down some of the HAs. They aspirated (drew water off an elbow) without presence or permission of a doctor. That can become very complicated. Boy what some won't attempt to do… Funny the accidents all seem to happen at the same time in the yard and we either have a crowd or nothing doing. I guess I'll quit for now as they want the lights out. Good night, Walter."

September 30 - "Neil left the lab to me & a case came in, so I ran a slide on him and & diagnosed it correctly. I had Dr. Campbell confirm the reading. I believe I would enjoy that work."

Walter describes three instances of drunken corpsmen, DeVore among them. He and his wife are having problems. Later, DeVore and Walter go out for milkshakes and DeVore buys his mother a birthday card. DeVore is fortunate to have Walter for a friend and I think he knows it.

Walter does not get his letter in the mail that night, and the next day, October 1, he adds a page. "The other night I priced the fares home. $14 round trip by train, $23 one way by plane. It would be nice to fly home & return by train. I'm thinking about the 20th but don't plan on it…. Love Walter"

October 3 Walter begins his eighty-sixth letter but is immediately interrupted. He resumes the next morning. "It's a beautiful day in Bremerton! The birds would be singing if there were any here & I would be out running around if I were free." In other news, three barrage balloons erupt in flames after being struck by lightning, St. Louis is disposing of the Yankees in the World Series and a corpsman transfers to Sitka, Alaska, as a dental tech.

In his next letter, October 6, Walter relates an incident in the pharmacy where he fills prescriptions and runs various blood tests, often without direct supervision. "The Dr. from receiving ship wrote two prescriptions on one blank – both for narcotics & ordered 60 half-grain tablets of phenobarbital and I questioned the thing & took it to Rickard & the Commander came by & said not to issue them. Then the Dr. came up & looked at it & said he had made a mistake & rewrote it for 21." Walter pays close attention when narcotics are prescribed.

On October 11 he writes - "My I get tired of talking & listening to other fellows poking their head in the window and gabbing. Funny how these fellows come & ask me questions as if I were smart. I suppose I should be, having been here so long." Walter is aware of his limitations. "I could have had the pharmacy to run had I wanted to. Rickard asked me… but I was afraid of the job. Too many things I've never been up against yet…. We acquire doctors and lose them so fast I can't remember the names …two new last week." Walter closes, hopeful that he will be granted sufficient leave to allow him to travel back to the ranch for a visit before he is deployed.

October 14 -"What I am afraid of is that the Waves will move in before Green leaves. They are scheduled to take over most of the duties of the building including pharmacy & lab."

On October 18 Walter manages a post card. "Dear Folks, I plan on leaving Seattle about 9:00 P.M. the 21st. Rather disappointed that couldn't make better connections, as plans are now. Love, Walter."

The next day he will turn 24. In the eight months since he started corpsman's school, he has mastered the material and passed all the tests with excellent scores. He is qualified to suture a wound, splint a broken bone, give an injection, work in the hospital storeroom, prepare prescriptions, work in the ER, examine blood in the lab, and submit the myriad, arcane paperwork (in triplicate) that the Navy requires. He remains modest with a good sense of humor.

From October 21 to November 4, Walter uses his two weeks of leave to visit the ranch. I'm sure he was glad to see the family and enjoyed Myrtle's home cooked food. I wonder, though, how the place appeared to him? Did he miss having electric lights and indoor plumbing? He has spent ten months in San Diego and Seattle. He has rubbed elbows with hundreds of men, and a few women, of many backgrounds, races, and social strata. Does he see Myrtle and Pop as uneducated hicks? I can't be sure but compared to Bremerton the ranch may feel very backward.

On November 5, back from leave, he writes, "Well the place is nearly the same. Six new corpsmen – two 2/c & the rest HA2/c…. Everyone speaks as if they missed me – a good act on their part. I'll try to always do the same as it makes it easier to start in again…. I got back at a bad time – grounds inspection tomorrow, personnel Sat. and likely an air raid drill soon…. Must go & press my uniform now just wet brushed it but think it will pass if pressed."

Nov 9 - "I could send a present or even a card but I'm too lazy to go out & get it, so I'll just address this letter to you as a birthday greeting and many happy returns of the day." Back less than a week, Walter has slipped into his normal routine: "… got the blood for typing … turned in my course for PhM2c.They had a terrible wind …blew the ferries around, broke off trees, broke windows etc."

Nov 12 - "The new chief wanted me to be senior corpsman, but I talked myself out of it so I'm just ambulance driver." That is Walter's claim, but his next sentence says otherwise. "We had a bad day in the lab. Yesterday there were too many complete blood counts etc.… I will have it until Sat when Neil gets back. Boy, I'll be glad to give it back to him.

"Did I tell you DeVore turned into the hospital? He is being treated for trench mouth as it's so bad it has eaten away about a third of one tonsil.… I was up to see him and of course he was doing something that he wasn't supposed to – sitting on the sun porch with the rest of the patients when he was supposed to be in an isolation ward."

I wonder what goes through Myrtle's mind as Walter relates the on-going saga of Lloyd DeVore. DeVore seems to be a classic screw-up; a blackout drunk, brawling, late returning from leave, shirking his duties, and now potentially infecting other sailors with what sounds like a particularly nasty strain of trench mouth. Yet Walter looks out for DeVore, even lending him money. Does Myrtle wonder why?

In fact, though, DeVore is not the only borrower. "Rickard borrowed $5 from me & I had already lent 5 to another fellow so I'll have to cash my check pretty soon I guess." The Walter I knew was frugal and I wonder if he ever receives 'interest' of any kind on these loans. I can't imagine Walter as a loan shark, but he mentions that sometimes a man would pay him "a little extra".

November 15 - he has been studying when the body of a yard worker is brought in. Walter suspects a heart attack. Neil has returned, now a married man, and Walter hopes he will "settle down".

On November 18, in a short, cryptic letter, Walter mentions making his first blood draws, three of them, without trouble. Later he takes the ambulance out and picks up a "…girl that had a pain in her abdomen & went back to work after the Dr sent her home, so I had to go & get her a second time. Don't know what we'll do with her.… We have begun to ask if it has quit raining instead of 'how is the weather.' We need water wings."

November 21, Walter is in the lab. "It's getting so I sort of like it a little now. I looked for Malaria the other day – went to the hospital to run it. Also had the Dr. help me on an acid-fat-bacteria for tuberculosis... had it been positive there would have been almost no hope for the patient. Ran 2 Bogens and took a C.B.C. differential and sedimentation.... Dr. Peterson showed me an ear drum that had a hole in it.... He is very nice as most are. They all seem very willing to help whenever I ask."

Just over a month ago, when Walter was first assigned to work in the lab, he resisted. It would be too hard, he thought, too much to learn. Now he is functioning much like a civilian lab tech. The doctors have noticed his progress and go out of their way to mentor him. Walter still lacks confidence, but he is curious, and his natural ability allows him to master tasks and grasp medical knowledge quickly.

Most of the letter is about Walter's daily duties. However, changes are coming to the hospital. "Next Monday we will get a group of new corpsmen. Wish we wouldn't. We just pile up seems to me, but Mr. Rickard wants 'manpower' & I guess he has to train some men to replace us when we go." Even though he knows he cannot, Walter would like to remain in Bremerton.

"November 22, I don't know what to say about Byron. If his occupation is established, he won't have to go but possibly he won't have to go anyway because of physical condition. We always said we would give him the education." Myrtle has shared her worry that Byron, who has just turned 19, will be drafted. Walter can offer little solace and his focus is on his own situation. Chief Rickard "... gave me a folder to study, one intended for a Dr. who was transferred. Very good but an awful lot to learn."

I am impressed that Walter, who graduated from a one room rural grade school and received only slightly above average marks in high school, has learned so much so quickly. Chief Rickard is apparently impressed enough to challenge him with material intended for doctors.

Walter asks Myrtle to tell Cousin Dick not to put a lot of trust in a Marine recruiter's promises. "I'm afraid Dick can't expect any guarantee of school from the Marines. Once you're in the service all promises are forgotten. That often happens in the Navy."

The day before Thanksgiving, Walter writes that he and DeVore are the last two corpsmen from their original group. They are an unlikely pair – Walter, with an apparently unblemished record, trusted and respected by the Chiefs and Doctors, and near the top on all the tests, and DeVore – a work averse, binge drinker constantly in danger of being thrown in the 'Brig" for returning late from leave. Nevertheless, they have become close friends and when they take liberty together, DeVore remains sober. When Walter loans him money, DeVore pays it back.

Walter sounds positively gleeful about one patient. "Gave a Chief the works yesterday – everything except trench mouth & T.B. test. He came in with a sore toe & today he's in the hospital."

In his November 29 letter Walter includes the Navy's thanksgiving menu. Ranging from soup to nuts and finishing with cigars, the meal runs to twenty items. It includes ham, turkey, dressing, giblet gravy and sweet potatoes. Walter labels the menu as 'propaganda' and laments, "Too bad you couldn't have prepared this. It would have really been delicious. It was good – considering. The cake & and pie were excellent. Brought in three ambulance cases that evening – maybe too much dinner?"

Walter describes his Thanksgiving weekend. A relative drove up from Portland and induced Walter to join him on his return trip. They tried to visit Walter's Uncle Dan, but… "They weren't home, so we walked in & got stuff from the store & had supper ready for them when they arrived. Were they surprised to see me." Walter grew close to Uncle Dan, who is six years his senior, when Dan lived with them during their first years at the ranch, so Walter was comfortable dropping in unannounced in Portland.

The next day Dan gave Walter a tour of the Portland shipyards and later, Dan's shop. When it was time to return to Bremerton, things did not go as Walter expected. "We headed out for the bus depot & ended up at the airport where Dan had made reservations for me. Was I surprised."

Unfortunately, Walter's first plane ride was rough. "I was quite sick at times but held it down. It was very nice up high but coming down it was like riding a bucking horse. I'd like to try it again on a good day."

The next evening, Walter is back at work. By now he is familiar with hospital operations and can do most anything that doesn't require a doctor. Besides his medical skills, he has become adept at navigating the stormy sea of BUMED[1] paperwork.

During his time at Bremerton, Walter has grown closer to his relatives in the area. He has made multiple visits to Marymoor Farm where his cousins, aunts and uncles have always made him welcome.

Walter's December 3 letter is cheerful. He has been Christmas shopping and the folks' presents are on the way. He has the lab ready for inspection and is unworried. He reminds his family, "Don't open those packages till Xmas. Love to all, Walter."

"December 5... this afternoon and tomorrow I have the pharmacy to take care of.... Well we passed another inspection – as usual. This captain isn't tough enough to my notion. We had good fruitcake for Thanksgiving – made me hungry for some that you used to have.

"I heard one I want to repeat before I forget it. Sailor from Texas looked up into the perpetual rain & saw the balloons floating as usual and said, 'Why don't they cut them loose and let this place sink?' Goodnight"

Sunday December 6 Walter writes that his course, the typed multi-page document of questions and answers required in order to be rated a PhM2c, has just earned him $2.50.

As large as the Navy is, in some ways it is like a quarrelsome family. "Johnson, one of our teachers in corps school, a PhM1c, came up here and the other day he flew off the handle as he often did down there & called the chief some names. When he wouldn't control himself after the chief warned him, the chief put him on report. Now he is a prisoner-at-large (P.A.L.), awaiting a court martial proceedings. He had taken his chief exam & was waiting for an opening. Now he will probably be broken to 2/c. No one seems to feel sorry for him."

---

[1] US Navy Bureau of Medicine and Surgery

On December 9 Walter notes the aftereffects of the extraction of his two impacted wisdom teeth. "My chin is a dimple & my mouth a small hole. Fun watching the doctors – they don't recognize me at first." He has been laid up, unable to work for days, and the other corpsmen have assumed his duties. "The fellows have been awfully good – bring me stuff & take care of me swell." By that evening he is recovering. "After another Epsom salts soak & 2 hrs. sleep, I feel pretty good & the swelling is going down slightly."

Saturday, Dec 12 - "Dear Folks, I'm not sending them (the many relatives) any presents just Christmas cards. I don't know how to buy for them.

"Rickard called me in yesterday & started getting excited about our rates. Guess I will take the test for 2c the 20th & be rated first of year." Walter assumes his rerating to PhM2c will go as planned.

"Our dinner today was the first time since Tuesday breakfast I've been to chow. Had mashed potatoes, soup, and some pie filling…. I've lived on milk shakes. I've never been hungry but lost 12 pounds – not in the face. Boy the dentists tell me to keep away from up there bad for business…. I'm coming out in technicolor now. The swelling is practically gone but I can't close my mouth yet. Never has been sore."

Walter is back on duty. "Rickard offered me 4 days leave but I told him the week-end after Christmas would do just as well. I'll go over to Marymoor…. Tonight I have to act as senior corpsman. That's not too bad, but Kersey says when I make 2c he is going to put me on the chief watch. That will mean that only the officer of the day will be over me …. really, I don't care for the prospect. I've been here too long. They start depending on me too much." It is clear that while Walter doesn't mind working, supervising others is still a struggle.

Walter has met all kinds of people in the Navy, men like Antoine Tabor, a Cajun, whose boyhood was even more primitive than Walter's. "From Louisiana – has been telling us about back home. He says back in the wood country there are towns of 400 or 500 where 99% of the people have never heard an English word. Everything is French." Tabor describes them as ignorant of trains, radio etc. and very mistrustful of outsiders. "He's ¾ Indian and French – very interesting – speaks very fast & jerky – nervous – heavy 195 -5'5" rather dark. Not often we can get him to talk much. Most talk too much & spin it as they go along."

December 16, Walter lists the gifts he has sent and describes his day in the lab. "Just reading your letter – little use giving me advice (about his mouth) because before you hear about anything and have the advice to me, I'm well." Myrtle may be loath to accept that with his medical training, Walter is no longer a little boy with a skinned knee who needs her home remedies.

December 19 - His test for PhM2c has been delayed till Monday, so he goes to the movies. "I went out to see the supposedly great picture 'Bambi.' I was terribly disappointed. The nurses fixed up a tree & decorated it. Now they have placed some boxes in there for the corpsmen. Guess we'll have to chip in & buy them something. They're going to use the 2nd deck for W.A.V.E.S. quarters.

"Christmas is in the air & they are getting in the mood. You know before I joined the Navy, I couldn't tell a drunk unless he was laid out. Now I can spot him pretty well. We have a couple corpsmen who never draw a sober breath – wonder how they keep going."

Walter is frustrated by the delayed test, disappointed by 'Bambi,' and disgusted by the drunks. Now he is dreading the arrival of the W.A.V.E.S. As he writes, "Guess they're really going to come – and the complications will follow." Poor Walter, this is no doubt his first Christmas away from home and it shows. He puts the letter away for the night, unfinished.

The next morning, a Sunday, he gives the office a good cleaning, even scrubbing the walls. Work, his 'go to' solution for nearly any problem, has improved his attitude and he is able to close without further complaints. "I haven't had anything to do today yet – strange… I guess I'll go & read the funny paper & the Post. Nothing more to say. May I wish you all a very Merry Christmas. Love to all. Walter."

Around this time, Walter sent the family three separate Christmas cards. David, now seven, received his own envelope addressed to Master David A. Dodd. None of the three cards bear any religious symbol – no wise men or angles, no Baby Jesus, and no scripture.

On December 22, because of the holiday, Walter is very busy in the lab. He has mentioned running Kahn tests and G.C. slides without identifying the purpose of either. The Kahn test is for syphilis and I wonder if G.C. stands for Gonorrhea Culture. Walter has completed two of three parts of his PhM2/c test and shows no concern about his score.

The hospital resembles a waystation. Corpsmen, nurses, patients, and doctors come and go. Every day their faces change, while in the background 'White Christmas' plays on an endless loop. Two corpsmen Walter finds particularly irritating, Ericson (spoiled rich kid), and Bamber (too stubborn for his own good), are due to be deployed, and I laugh to read Walter's special Christmas wish for them. "I hope he and Bamber are sent to some station or ship where everything is very Navy – strictly regulation."

Walter notices an influx of female patients. "My, but there are getting to be an awful lot of women patients in E.C.C. now. Seems like they're ill or getting sprained ankles all of the time. It would help a lot if they would wear sensible shoes."

After spending the better part of a page describing a new x-ray machine that will cost about $20,000, Walter grouses a bit about "…a bum haircut today…" that probably cost about a quarter.

He is unimpressed by the Seattle winter so far. "Oh, yes that little snowfall or heavy frost a while back – poo. Maybe I'll see some Alaska snow though, mustn't speak too soon. I'm going to try to get over to the farm over the week-end. Love to all & all a good night, Walter."

It is Christmas Eve, a few hours before midnight, and naturally Walter is at the desk. One corpsman has suffered an attack of appendicitis and the others are off duty, so he is the sole, as well as the senior, corpsman. He is pleased though because "… I have received 2 presents – Second Class Pharmacist Mate as of Jan. 1 … and a package from Si & Rose, swell box of caramels." He has achieved his new rank but has no time to revel in it.

"Two drunk sailors in. Both had their hands well skinned & their clothes & their 2 Marine escorts' clothes were messed. They'd been punching windows out with their bare hands, lots of nervous excitement today." Later, the drunk sailors disposed of, Walter takes time to thank Myrtle. "Mother this is a swell pocketbook. I've already transferred all of my possessions into it. I won't cut the cake for a while because there is so much going around, I wouldn't enjoy it."

The next morning Walter continues his letter. "Well it is Christmas and I'm Senior Corpsman, slave driver & what-not. All but 14 men went ashore. I traded today for tomorrow." The day is young, things are quiet, and Walter is in a reflective mood. "Rickard has gone so I'm left alone here in the office. I'll be making something like $96 a month now – about as much as the farm?"

Walter is right about the farm. The farm's tax returns for the war years did not survive, but based on a scattering of bills and receipts, the farm would have been fortunate to clear $96 a month. Most of their income would have been from sales of eggs, cream, wool, and any lambs not killed by coyotes. In the early 1950s, I remember we ate a lot of mutton because, Dad said, an old ewe was only worth about $5 at auction.

Still writing on Christmas Day, Walter continues, "You know I can't help but notice the difference between Marines and Sailors. The Marines are so much better behaved – no fooling around & boy do they jump when the sergeant speaks…. Boy that would be tough duty." In a few months Walter will revise parts of this assessment.

Walter passes on a piece of news and then closes. "Quite a headline – Darlan killed, just a few more I could think of & it would help out a lot. Love to all, Walter."

Although he seldom mentions the war, Walter stays informed. Francois Darlan, a French admiral and later a minister in the Vichy government, collaborated with Hitler and at one point worked for the defeat of the British. Darlan changed sides more than once and on the afternoon of December 24, 1942, he was assassinated – shot by a 20-year-old youth. On December 26, Darlan's killer faced a firing squad.

That same day, Walter is off to Marymoor Farm and on Monday the 29th he writes a long letter, his last of the year. "Dear Folks, Well, I spent a very pleasant week-end at the farm…. Seems they always go to an awful lot of trouble for me though. We always have a big dinner

74

at Gert's and they all come…. 16 at dinner." Walter receives more presents, some that he neither needs nor wants. Everyone is good to him,
to the point of embarrassment. In all his holiday celebrations Walter has
forgotten his parent's 25th anniversary. He is chagrined and struggles to
make up for his failure.

"Mom, I'm so sorry I forgot your wedding anniversary and it's your
silver one too…. What shall I get you? I can buy something thru ships
service at a great reduction & have plenty of money to get anything you
want – up to $75 outside price. Just let me know size, kind, pattern,
color or whatever necessary."

January 3, 1943 - "Dear Folks, I've written so many letters in the
past few days – at least 4 – that I should have made carbon copies, so
I'd know who I said what to."

Walter has been a PhM2/c for three days. "You know I'm ashamed
to wear my 2/c crow because I know I don't know what I'm supposed
to…. Guess I'll have to work into it as I did my 3/c." 'Crow' is navy
slang for petty officer rank insignia which features an eagle (crow) above
one to three chevrons, depending on rank.

Walter describes a New Year's Eve party where "… the host got very
drunk … I had Coca Cola." He starts to relate a dream about being back
on the ranch and interrupts himself in mid sentence – "Must replenish
my A.P.C. stock now." The pharmacist has week-end liberty, and he has
been drafted by Rickard to fill in. "He calls me his old standby – just
flatters me to keep me on the job I guess."

Over an hour later, the capsules made up, Walter continues. "Just
finished…. Lewis (Lewy) was in & helped with the capsules just for the
experience …. He's one of the funniest, strangest fellows one will ever
meet. He acts to me like inbred – but he's smart at book learning and
a pretty nice fellow… You know so far it seems that the fellows haven't
resented my making the rate. So often they say that you're 'flashing your
rate' etc." Walter thanks Myrtle again for the pocketbook she sent and
closes his letter.

Walter has finished his first year in the Navy and his letters reveal a
young man amused by the absurdities of life, and modest about his own

abilities. He is grateful for the kindness he receives, civil even to those he doesn't like, and eager to gain new knowledge. Sometimes moody, but always hardworking, he is silently critical of any man who doesn't do his job. He describes another corpsman, who has since be transferred, as "… a big fat slob that dragged his feet and was very dumb."

For a teetotaler, Walter has become more tolerant of drunks – as long as they do their jobs. He is biased against Texans, who he sees as loud and arrogant. He still doubts the wisdom of having women in the military. "This morning a W.A.V.E. officer called up to see if she could get her throat sprayed here. The Chief said it was OK … I'm afraid we will run into many complications."

January 10 is a quiet Sunday and Walter is working the desk, answering the phone and, of course, writing letters. His brief letter to brother David is made of short, simple sentences and the subject matter is kid friendly – snow, skis, school, and the shortage of chewing gum. David's letter is in its own envelope, which costs Walter nothing because he is using ink, paper, and envelopes provided by the Navy, and as to postage, he simply writes 'free' in the area normally reserved for a stamp, and the Navy and the USPS do the rest.

Walter's relationship with his family is complex. Byron, though five years younger, is loud and assertive, and he and Walter are natural rivals. It is hard to overstate Walter's closeness to Myrtle, but Pop is another story. Albert is volatile, and prone to go from morose to furious in a heartbeat. Myrtle's letters act as a lifeline to his family and the world Walter knew before the Navy took hold of his life.

January 14 – Three weeks after Christmas, Walter is still catching up with thank you letters and enjoying the Seattle winter, which he says, "… feels like June just before a rain.

"A new man came in yesterday … Rasansky, a Polish Jew, I guess. Don't know why but there is quite a bit of resentment against him. Some because he's a Jew … he is fresh out of lab school in Maryland…. In here he acts as though he could take over and we have to check practically all he does because we don't agree with his results. A doctor called him wrong twice yesterday."

Walter shares a tale from a man just back from action in the Pacific. "Talked today to a PhM1/c who …survived a torpedoing that killed 5 men, one no more than 5 feet from where he was standing. Sub fired at them on a very stormy night – 2 fish – storm diverted one, & they took the other amidships, & really wrecked parts of it…. They beached the ship & poured concrete in the hole & came here for repairs…. They – mine sweepers – got the sub the next day… with depth charges… a destroyer came along with the 5" gun & sank her. Saw pictures of the prisoners in a magazine."

Walter writes that he was in the lab "… showing a couple fellows how to do C.B.C. & in came 3 Bogens one right after the other…. Before I got the reports typed, Bamber came back from …Tacoma with an officer that the Hospital wouldn't accept because the proper papers weren't made out down there. For some strange reason I took it upon myself to get him in instead of leaving it up to the Chief or the Senior Corpsman a PhM2/c. I got him in O.K. but knew some of it wasn't right…. Rickard said this morning it wasn't bad – a couple minor mistakes but he's in which is the important part."

Walter has again violated the Navy's axiom "Never volunteer for anything." It would have been easier to pass the buck but that was not his nature. Seeing the man needed to be hospitalized, Walter put the patient's welfare over bureaucratic rules and made it happen. Whether he is filling out forms in Bremerton or bandaging wounded Marines on an island in the Pacific, Walter will act with initiative.

On the subject of money he writes, "Funny you said I would have more money with my pay increase. I've always had all I needed." He feels others gain nothing from promotions because they just spend more. "So nothing is really gained – perhaps a little harder on their health." Partying is not for him. "I think this year I would rather put most of my money into improvements on the ranch … something that will be valuable after the 'emergency'."

January 17 - "It's a beautiful day in Bremerton. Last night the thermometer went down to 20 & the wind blew just like Missoula. Ice around the streets, cars frozen up and the sun out beautifully.

"I just picked up a girl at a shop who apparently had fainted. Brought her in here, warmed her up and then they took her home…. Two new girls have been hired here… I believe Chief Smith's Coke business will boom because they both seem to enjoy them, with a group…. Last night I went out & saw 'The Black Swan,' a buccaneer story … much too crude & rough for my liking. Carrying off women, blowing up ships, piercing each other with swords etc.

"A girl was brought in this morning for a Bogens test by an officer. She was fighting, cursing, and crying. From her badge picture she must be quite attractive… We just made out the report & let the officer have her…. It's a terrible sight though." Walter is no longer a naïve boy, fresh from the farm, but his ideas about the proper role of women are old fashioned. The war has changed a woman's 'place' in American society, and the WAVES and Rosie the Riveter have become the new norm.

Despite his reservations about women in the Navy, Walter admits that the Navy policy on drunks is unfair. Men, and DeVore is a classic example, are forgiven multiple times for drunken misbehavior while "… the women are kicked out upon first offense."

By January 19, the base is under over a foot of snow which is still coming down. "No one is prepared & they are all stuck so besides not having chains they don't know how to drive.

"This was payday & …all wanted to go out but the gas & electricity are both out in Bremerton so they couldn't do a thing. They're all back now – going to play poker with their money."

One of the corpsmen had liberty and planned to go home. "Trying to get away from the dispensary he got stuck & not a soul would go out and help him. He's generally not very well liked – too much stuck on himself – his wife – his things etc."

Another corpsman, Nichols, is in real trouble. "He jumped ship. Came in overdue & generally messed around and was punished, but he went too far. He was restricted so had his girl come into the yard. The police picked them up for necking & Nichols threatened the police … so they added that…. He may get kicked out of the Navy if he isn't careful.

"I'm getting on with the new fellow better now just found he was overanxious to work. He taught me one new thing so far.

"Nothing new to write. I'm sending my check. I believe it would be better to spend it for something like shingles for the shed or machinery – save it towards a tractor rather than bonds."

Things are slow at the dispensary, but "…night before last Red, the senior corpsman, needed help so called me – couldn't find morphine & needed help on a stretcher so I got up at midnight and helped take the man out to the hospital."

January 27 - "I told you Nichols was A.W.O.L…. today he was placed on P.A.L. roster (prisoner at large) …. Made two ambulance trips today – one to pick up a … drug addict – phenobarbital and the other a 400 lb. lady (almost) that fell down some stairs & skinned her shins.

"A 1/c reported in a few days ago from somewhere in the South Pacific. Seems to be a pretty good sort. Don't know where he will work but he … has had considerable 1st aid in actual combat. Haven't heard him say (boast) much about it yet so perhaps I'll believe what he does say."

Walter's financial report is more detailed than usual. "I find I have $18 lent out so far this payday, collected 2 today & lent 3. That would be swell if I collected interest…. Wonder how much I'll have out when I get my orders & then how much I'll collect of it."

He hasn't heard from Neil in weeks and seems hurt – "I know it's hard for him to write letters but surely he should write at least once in a while."

Apparently, Myrtle hasn't written for a while either, which Walter blames on the weather. "When you folks get out of hibernation you might drop me a line. Love Walter."

By February 1st, when Walter writes again, his speculation that his folks were snowbound has been confirmed. Three letters from Myrtle arrive over just a couple days. Something else is new – the Dodd's have a new address, P.O. 618. General Delivery is a thing of the past and their mail is now available seven days a week with no standing in line. They will keep that post office box for fifty years.

He has finally heard from Neil, who is unhappy as usual, though not without reason. He is stationed on Adak while Paloma, his young wife, remains behind. Walter is better off at Bremerton where he can do his job in his sleep – and nearly does – "I need a shower and some sleep, so I'll close now & write you again Sunday.... Love Walter.

"February 5, Dear Folks. This was pay day & I'm sending the check along.... Nichols and Crane were shipped out today – Boy was Rickard elated.... Today I found I will never see 'my' W.A.V.E. in the lab – she won't arrive until July.... I've got to go & holler at the pay office. I'm sure I'm about $20 behind in my pay ... the way I figure. WED."

On February 9, Walter stands his first watch in the new building. The place is quiet, so he has time to write about all sorts of things. He covers medications and their uses, the outstanding performance of their Jeep in the snow, and the amazing accuracy of Uncle Ralph's palm reading. He ponders the lambing prospects on the ranch, laughs about a six-page letter from Mrs. Pope, who "talks a lot but doesn't say much", and laments the broken mainspring on his less than a year-old watch.

February 13 - "Slagh, a PhM2/c is just back from Guadalcanal via Mare Island Hospital. He has seen the worst the Japs could dish out and has told some real action stories. He isn't one to brag or spin yarns. He was at Henderson Field when the Japs got within 50 feet... The artillery is what saved the place. I guess he must have broken – nerves. He never said, but that's what we gathered. Seems OK now. A great many of the fellows do.... He spoke of his last days there when he was on a hillside... several of the foxholes were covered up by shells and bombs but in his sector, he only lost one man that night – smothered - ... others dug out in time. They don't take soldiers as prisoners often.... Usually they *(the Marines)* shoot the wounded *(Japanese soldiers)* rather than try to bring them to medical attention. I rate the weekend but feel too bad to take it." I don't think Walter is actually ill. Slagh's stories show Walter an ugly, potential future. Before this letter Walter has spared his family any detailed description of the war from a corpsman's perspective.

The rest of this letter is lighter, filled with jokes, observations of local fauna, silly rumors, family information and even another movie review.

He adds a postscript: "Gee I get a kick out of the fellows sometimes. Clausen is trying to get me to learn to swear. Canverse would like to see how I'd react in an air raid. 'You are always so cool.' It makes me laugh."

February 16 Walter writes his final letter from Bremerton. "Thursday I'm being transferred South. Likely to Frisco. Rather disappointed because I'd talked & planned so much on Alaska – maybe they'll still send me there – suppose?" Walter picked the Navy over the army when he enlisted because he preferred to risk a quick death at sea to the chance of being killed or maimed for life in a land battle. At that time Japan had not attacked Alaska, and duty there likely seemed preferable to serving in a steamy, snake-filled jungle, with a sniper lurking behind every tree.

Walter won't be traveling alone. Heese, Coffman, Erikson, Ellis, Munski, Knode and, of course, DeVore are moving as well. "Boy is this hurting Rickard because he is already short of men." Walter takes some consolation from the fact that Rasansky is staying behind. Walter has struggled to get along with Rasansky who 'acts like he could take over the lab' but whose test results 'we have to check.' Walter does not single out other 'Jews' or voice any objection to the Jewish religion, so his problem is with the man. Walter is never meanspirited, but with Rasansky he comes close. "At least now I'm getting away from this Jew though. He's crying because he'll have to do all the work & can't get any help. Wish I could watch him cry."

Bremerton has been good duty for Walter, and he has enjoyed it. Even as he leaves, he tries to reassure his family. "Love to all, Walter. Don't worry about me I'll be enjoying myself I'm sure."

At 1540, on February 18, Walter takes the ferry to Seattle and catches the overnight train to Portland. There, facing a long layover, he manages to send a penny postcard. "Dear Folks, Here at Portland…. Went out to Dan's but no one home – have 4 more hrs. to kill…. Love Walter."

That night, at 2100 hours, he is rolling south on the Southern Pacific. "Dear Folks, … I hope and pray for a speedy delivery from San Francisco. If I had my choice of the fellows going with me from this group, I'd pick DeVore to handle the men and circumstances, Munski to keep up the morale, Rhodes for efficiency & work, Herb for work, although Herb and Lloyd go on some bad drunks together." Walter has unconsciously adopted the point of view of the group's leader. "My but some of the boys paid me some wonderful compliments when I left & I know that most of them were sincere. Never will forget what Canverse told me. A couple of the boys nearly cried when we left."

One of his precautions is something an actual leader might do. "Because I didn't want Knode drunk to start the trip, Munski & I took care of him." He describes how, with time to kill, they take Knode to a Swedish Smorgasbord on 7th and Pike where they stuff themselves for $1.50 before taking in a movie. Finally, at 2330 their train pulls out of Seattle. Knode is presumably still mostly sober.

After laying over in Portland the next day, they reboard, and Walter writes, "Tonight I'm sleeping in a lower berth for the first time.... Darn I've got too much money with me – better than $70 when I started.... Darn but most of these fellows drink far too much when traveling. None of our gang have done anything yet – a swell group. We're finally rolling & fast. Think I'll read till I fall asleep.... Goodnight, Walter."

PART 4 – CAMP ELLIOTT – 20 LETTERS,
FEBRUARY 20, 1943 – APRIL 25, 1943

Walter's next letter, dated Sunday, February 21, describes his arrival at the Treasure Island Naval Base in the San Francisco Bay. "Arrived in Oakland at 2100. Then reported to Frisco – walked 6 blocks & they sent us to Goat Island. They sent us to Treasure Island at 2300 … didn't have any baggage so we pulled down some cots and slept under our raincoats…. This morning DeVore started out after the bags. We got them at 1400…. A Lt. fixed us up with a truck and Munski, Lloyd and I went to Oakland & picked them up. Boy but traffic travels here… those street cars don't stop most of the time – people land on the run & the noise is terrific.

"I feel swell now, just took a shower & put on clean clothes…. The chow was swell here today & the canteen large & nice. It should be a swell place if we get a good detail." How quickly things change: less than 48 hours ago, Walter had "… prayed for a speedy delivery from San Francisco".

"Fun listening to the boys gripe – but this is nice & believe I'll enjoy myself for at least 2 weeks if they don't work me too hard." The Marines have other plans and allow Walter a single week.

Walter is overwhelmed. "Enough men in there to make one dizzy to watch." He asks Myrtle not to write him for a while and ends with "This is a pretty place, site of the World's Fair you know. Love, Walter"

Treasure Island is quite impressive. The island was constructed beginning in 1937. Located just north of the Bay Bridge, it was built by placing many tons of rock atop preexisting shoals and covers 400 acres. By 1939, the 'Magic Isle' was open for business with multiple fairgrounds, exhibit halls, and two large hangars for sea planes. The island was intended to become a second airport for San Francisco, but after the War came, the Navy seized the island, declaring it essential to the war effort. By the time Walter arrived Treasure Island was operating as a reception station where up to 12,000 sailors and Marines were processed each day for assignment in the Pacific. The crowding and chaos would have been bewildering to a newcomer and Walter was plunged headlong into this maelstrom.

On February 22, Walter writes his second letter from the island. "Dear Folks, Here I am …not that I have much to say but I do have an address…. I'm working in the post office… So many fellows have the same name & initials. Today two fellows had identical names & rates except one's middle name was Lee & the other Leo. Lloyd just came in & found that someone had swiped his mattress, blanket & pillow…. Guess tomorrow I'll lock my blankets up – they're too good to lose."

Despite the problem with thievery, things don't look all bad. "Duty should be good, here better chow than up there & always plenty – milk – eggs – meat – butter…. I'm turning in early tonight – don't feel too well – a sort of a cold…."

On February 25 Walter sorts the mail "…from 0800 until it is done, which is rather tiresome … liberty every night. Last night Lloyd & I went to S.F. & caught the first streetcar from the station & rode out to the park & saw a swanky looking restaurant so stopped in. We'd heard you couldn't buy meat for love or money, but he got half a chicken & I got 2 very nice lamb chops for 80 cents – full dinner. Then … caught a car back to town."

Friday is Walter's last night on Treasure Island, and Saturday, February 27, he goes with DeVore, Munski and Heese, to Goat Island where they are ordered to report to the Marines on Monday. Free for the weekend and with their Navy housing gone "… we went ashore & rented a double room at the Y.M.C.A. - $1.60."

The four corpsmen wander through China Town, fascinated by the sights and the exotic inhabitants. They browse Chinese curio shops where the people chattered in 'chink,' meet a 'Jew' who offers to buy DeVore's diamond ring for a tenth of its true value, and encounter Italians with wine and garlic for sale. Today Walter's words would be considered racist, but they contain no malice and in 1943 were accepted and in common usage by many, perhaps most, white Americans.

Next the four fellows take in a "very good movie" and then catch a streetcar to an Oyster House on Market street where they have a "swell" meal for $1.03. Sunday night, before they board their train for the overnight ride to San Diego, Walter notes, "Treasure Island is swell. Goat terrible. The bridge over it & the noise is terrific." None of them know what is ahead.

San Diego, March 2 - "Dear Folks, right now I'm writing on a school desk because of all things I'm going back to school only this time I'm a Marine. This is a permanent change of station."

For Myrtle, this would be, in Walter's words, "a terrible shock." Her oldest son, who she has depended on the most, is now the property of the US Marines, a group renowned for their aggressive, bloody, battles. I expect her first reaction was some combination of fury and despair. Walter's situation is rich with irony. His previous comments about Marines – at one point he referred to Marines in general as 'bums' – have been negative, and now he is one of them.

His letter continues. "Thursday we are to be issued Marine clothes & have rifle firing – get pistols tomorrow. Certainly was surprised to draw this for duty – no medical training just how to take care of oneself. Believe I'll have a picture taken of myself in Marine uniform …. Munski calls the bright blue uniform a 'rainbow at attention'." After this weak attempt at levity, Walter tries to look on the bright, or at least the less dark, side.

"Just back from chow. Because I'm 2/c I eat with the sergeants & they sit down to a table all set with plates and food. Privates and rookies keep the tables supplied – waiters. Good food and plenty of it. Certainly nice to serve one's self.... Love to all from your Marine. Walter".

Walter's March 5 letter is from Camp Elliott, a Marine training base on a mesa north of San Diego. "Dear Folks, believe you've disowned me but then I don't blame you – haven't heard from you since I wrote & told you I'd been Shanghaied.... Tonight we had to stand & sing the Marine Hymn. Don't expect regular letters from me now. I can't even think straight.

"Today we fired 72 rounds of M1's." Walter describes the firing exercise in detail before moving on to his struggle to get all the accessories of a true Marine. He will face his first inspection without a field scarf, or emblems, both of which he must purchase himself. As Walter writes, "It costs money to become a Marine." Even after he purchases a barracks cap, he will have to pay to get his trousers shortened. "Today was payday for Marines but they passed me by – hard on me - $47.10 left. Rich compared to most fellows. Gosh but I'm glad I'm 2/c – can't get over it, we eat at tables & almost rate like humans." Walter, determined to put a good face on his new situation, restates the only benefit of life with the Marines - the corpsmen don't have to stand in chow lines.

"My right ear is almost deaf... shoulder a little red, legs & feet fine – not a bad physical report eh? Forgot my appetite which is also very good. Should see Lloyd now – he's putting on weight looks better & feels 100% better since he quit drinking.... Love Walter".

Despite the pace of the training, Walter writes again March 9. "From now on we have about 8 classes ...Every day we will have some drill & Thurs we're scheduled for the 15-mile hike and we'll have to set up first aid stations."

When he can Walter takes liberty, either to watch out for Lloyd or for some other reason. "They intend to take me to the movie tonight ... I'm tired of movies ... have seen too much of Hitler." I've got to get a filling in my tooth, it's beginning to bother. Back from the picture – a waste of time.... Lots I could say. The camouflage work here is wonderful.... Wishing you a happy birthday Dad -... love Walter."

March 13, a Saturday, Walter takes time to sort out the mass of letters he has received. Some have been delayed and many are out of order. "I have 4 of your letters here. Have written since two came but didn't read as I wrote so didn't destroy them." (Letters from home are destroyed to prevent them from falling into enemy hands if a soldier is killed or captured.)

If he wants to, Walter can fill a page without saying much. Myrtle is unhappy Walter is with the Marines, and all Walter knows to do is make light of his assignment. "Funny you're not overjoyed upon my appointment to the Marines. Just think now I have two uniforms, better than most fellows can boast." With that, Walter changes the subject to inoculations and their after-effects - a topic always good for a distraction.

Although Walter and his fellow corpsmen don't know it, they are part of a master plan intended to counter Japanese activities in the Pacific. At the heart of this plan is the creation of a new Division - the Fourth Marines. The formation and training of the Fourth Marines began early in 1943 and will take the rest of the year. Most division elements are organized and grouped at Camp Lejeune, North Carolina. 'Organized' in this instance involves splitting some units, combining others, and building some from scratch. Beginning in early July, the east coast units will gradually move to Camp Pendleton and on August 16th, 1943, the 4th Division will be formally activated.

All this is yet to come. As of March 1943, Camp Pendleton, 45 miles north of Camp Elliott, is still under construction. For the next two months, the Marine Corps will train Walter at Camp Elliott to follow the Marines into battle so he can care for them when they are shot, bayonetted, blown to pieces, and otherwise damaged. When the trainers are satisfied, Walter will be transferred to Camp Pendleton.

Walter continues his March 13 letter. "Just finished a washing instead of going to chow. Have put in 4 hours of class today." He lists a movie, and one hour each of marching, communications, and litter drill, this last being postponed. Nothing sounds mentally taxing compared to his medical training.

"Meadow larks sing down here…. Bought a little gadget for you, Mom, to wear." Walter has picked up what he calls a "Kadusa" which, from his description is probably a caduceus of some design. "It really isn't just right for you but it's very close." Walter may be trying to mollify Myrtle's upset at his new status as a Marine, and I am struck by how much closer he is to Myrtle than to his father. Contrast this gift to his mother, which is for no particular occasion, with this comment drawn from his March 9th letter: "I'm not going to Diego before Dad's birthday so likely won't send a card.

Walter continues, "DeVore & a couple others are going on a real drunk this week." DeVore has been sober since coming to Camp Elliott, and Walter has known it wouldn't last. He seems resigned.

"Camp Elliott, March 21, Dear Folks…. I spent the week end with Davis's – a nice quiet time but I believe I enjoyed it more than going to La Jolla. They must be quite rich – the more I see of them the more they seem to have although they don't 'put on.' She has a Cadillac for her use, he has a Ford." Mrs. Davis is Myrtle's first cousin and she and her husband live in San Diego where they operate a laundry. The Davis's have taken to Walter, leaving him a bit in awe. "He offered to let me use his …car anytime I wished… meant it too." Walter will see them often throughout the year.

Walter's horizons continue to expand and in this letter, he introduces Yuska as "the fellow who bunks under me." Yuska, probably a Russian, is from the mining district around Scranton, PA. Walter explains that the young men "…were organized in gangs and had to stay, in order to live. Stole more than they got otherwise. … He has lived quite a life. Doesn't seem possible that there are so many parts to the U.S.A." I hear amazement, not judgement in Walter's words, and I am impressed by his ability to accept people who are so different than he. Having a common goal no doubt helps. Whether that goal is the defeat of Japan or simply surviving Marine basic training, he does not say.

In this 'under construction' division, two paydays have passed, and Walter has not been paid. He is down to $20 but tells Myrtle not to worry. He is holding $50 for DeVore and things will work out.

March 24, he writes, "Tonight I went down and sent off my sea bag … sent it collect so you take some money out of my check if I ever get one…. My finances are down to $18 … a little over a month now since my last one…. You know Dad or Byron could use my pea coat … also the raincoat…. Perhaps I'll never need them again so use all of them you can." Walter is adapting to reality. When (not if) he goes to sea in the Pacific, his heavy Navy wool pea coat will become a burden. Rather than lose it he will send it home. Later, in the 1960's, I will wear it and be right in style.

Sunday, March 28, Walter writes again. He started the 15-mile hike with a bad cold but managed to finish. Afterward, with a fever of 102, he checked in at the Dispensary. A day later his fever is down, and he feels well enough to write. "Haven't heard from Ruby and John (Myrtle's sister and her husband) since I've been here so I think I'd better write them. Your Marine, Walter".

When Walter writes again on April 3, he has been at Camp Elliott for a month. He tells no jokes and sounds discouraged. His fever is gone but he is still weak and worries it may return. He has seen a list of men killed in action and found one with the last name of Dodd. He wonders if they are related. He is late picking up his photos and bemoans the price. "You can't get anything cheap."

Fed up with Marines, he complains - "I get very tired of hearing the boot Marines brag about their branch of the service … I can see why they're not very popular." The expression 'boot Marine' is used to describe a Marine who has just finished basic training in 'boot camp' and is yet to be deployed. It is not a compliment.

Boot camp is taking its toll on the recruits. "Fellow next to me is in terrible shape. First, he fractured his elbow, 3 ribs & hurt his knee … then he got food poisoning. Now they tell him he has rheumatic fever. His joints get very sore & stiff…. Only one corpsman to look after over 50 patients." Presumably, the fellow with rheumatic fever will be given a medical discharge, though Walter never mentions it.

Walter tries to encourage his family. "You are doing well with the lambs. Soon it will be chicks won't it? Glad you like the pin. If I feel

OK, I'll go down and get my pictures... they bother me laying down there overdue.... Love, Walter".

Life at Camp Elliott is not easy for Walter and he struggles to adjust to the classes and field exercises. At Bremerton he provided useful medical treatment, and on liberty he visited with family. The countryside was green and beautiful. Here, in the middle of a desert, most of his fellow corpsmen have other assignments. He likes the Davises, but misses his uncles, aunts, and cousins. At Camp Elliott, instead of suturing wounds or working in the lab, he memorizes the organizational chart of the Marines. He forces himself to finish fifteen-mile hikes, while battling a lingering respiratory illness. His next assignment is a mystery, known only to the Marines, and he is caught in the doldrums.

April 7 - "Received your letter & guess I'll answer.... Still haven't been paid but have $10 left so think I'll make out." Walter is still weak, but he shows interest in things back home. After asking about the Shaughnessy's, an Irish family that lives five miles down the road, he fires a couple more questions. "No one moved into the Schramm place eh? Byron should be able to tend the lambs with David's help shouldn't he, leaving the housework & kids for you?

"A friend of DeVore said we were lucky to be with them – Marines – said it was good duty. Well perhaps but dispensary duty suits me better.... Darn but it's been doing a lot of raining here, the ground is soft. Athletes foot has broken out on me again." Walter mentions he has found his payroll records, which had been misfiled, and closes.

On April 11, he writes, "Boy I'm almost worn out, just finished 3 letters .... Still owe Dan, Marian, & Mrs. Davis – maybe they can wait awhile. Do you realize that I have only 2 more weeks of school?" Walter still has a bad cough, which may be why he feels so tired. He complains about the weather, but I would add homesickness. "Darn but it sounds terrible to hear you talk about the coming of spring. Here it's as cold as ever -believe I saw frost on the building roof although it may just have been heavy dew." Camp Elliot is only 350' above sea level, but to Walter, Southern California feels colder than the ranch.

Despite the weather, things are heating up as the corpsmen, used to the casual, almost benign atmosphere of the Navy's medical facilities, chafe under the rigid Marine discipline practiced at Camp Elliott. As Walter describes it, "This does seem to be a bad class. There are 10 men in the school on restriction and 6 are from this class."

Men are disciplined for smiling at the wrong time, and if challenged, the Marine Shore Patrol reacts with a brutality that surprises Walter. "Friday DeVore & Coffman went out together & got drunk. They split up about midnight and Coffman was picked up by the Shore Patrol – what for he didn't know. He said he wasn't doing anything - but did resist the S.P." Coffman was beaten badly and the next morning his appearance elicited a "Oh my God, what happened to you?" from an officer.

Walter continues, "Coffman was really a mess. The S.P. could get in trouble about that but likely won't. Hope they don't court martial Coffman & put him in the brig.... At PSNY Rickard would laugh at him & ... Captain Jewel would only reprimand him & perhaps restrict him for a week; this is different though; he must go before the colonel Mon. morning".

Apparently, Byron has been considering a move West in search of a higher paying job. "Byron shouldn't come to the coast. I have seen so many fellows going back home, Montana included, to $3.00 per day jobs because of the housing and the high living costs out here take everything away that they make." When Walter writes on April 14, he has news. "Munski & I are going to the Medical Company being formed. Lloyd is staying here as instructor.... He is not crazy about staying here. Funny very few want duty here of any sort.... Tomorrow we're scheduled for another hike & I've an idea we will take it. It's just possible they will gas us to see how we respond. Next week will be all tests.

"Got special pay Monday $140 so sending $100 along. Will draw $45 next Tuesday.... Think I'd better answer some more letters.... Saw Hellzapoppin Mon. Two or 3 parts were good. Love Walter"

Camp Elliott April 18 - It is Sunday and Walter is back after a weekend trip to L.A. with DeVore. When they were ready to start, the bus depot was closed so they began hitchhiking. Walter would not have dared the trip without DeVore. "I wanted to go with someone who could take care of himself." They were wearing their 'sailor suits' so getting rides was easy.

They saw the Brown Derby, Grauman's Chinese Theatre and Pershing Square. They "...stepped into the Post Office – very nice but didn't ride the escalator." In Hollywood Walter had one of his first experiences with black nightclub performers. The blind piano player was the main attraction, but the "...girls were enjoying themselves too much – spoiled their singing. I think they made up a lot of it as they went along." (From Walter's description the singers were improvising, or 'scatting' a popular style of the era). The ranch must have seemed far, far away.

Walter was impressed by a large amusement park – he calls it a 'playland' – where they rode a roller coaster that was "... much higher, faster, & longer than Seattle's." According to Walter, "I only spent about $6 for the whole thing – probably not that much."

Back at Camp Elliott, Walter writes that he will be moving to Pendleton in less than a week. Meanwhile, the final exams have begun, and Walter gets 100% on the first aid portion.

"Camp Elliott, April 22, ...Likely this will be the last letter I'll write from here. We finished our exams yesterday. Turned in our equipment so there's not much holding us." Walter scored 97 in First Aid, and 95 in Marine Organization and Chemical Warfare. Did Myrtle worry when she read Walter was being readied for Chemical Warfare?

Clothing is in short supply, especially shoes and hats, so Walter has become creative. "I found a pair of brown oxfords ... after some boys moved out & strangely, they fit. Cover them with black polish & wear them with my Marine clothes.... Still can't get an overseas hat to fit – not even in town – maybe I'll get one at Pendleton." Walter never states that he will be going into the Pacific with the Marines, but his reference to the 'overseas hat' should be a strong hint.

"Monday we were paid & Tuesday some of the boys were broke – 4 poker, 2 blackjack & a couple crap games in this one squad room. DeVore's made about $20 this time." Walter and DeVore have become even better friends, though one is a teetotaler and the other a binge drinker.

When Lloyd passes out, Walter looks out for him. "It's always my job to get him up so he can get the rest up. Always get an awful laugh watching him try to open his eyes & focus them."

Walter has received a letter from Myrtle's sister Ruby. "I feel very sorry for Ruby & John. She was wondering if there was any way I could be relieved so I could take care of their place. She's supposed to be in bed & John is in & out of the hospital. Surely too bad." I am stunned that Ruby could even imagine that the Marine Corps might release Walter for such a reason.

Myrtle may have asked Walter about the money he sends her, because he writes, "I don't care much what you do with the money – water pipe – tractor – bonds. Tractor would be very nice because we'd have that regardless of the value of the bonds after the war." Walter stops there, but the next day adds a page.

"Just heard we won't move *(to Pendleton)* till Monday, scuttlebutt & must be taken as such…. I'll miss Lloyd – he can furnish the brass where I lack it. I often wish I could act tough at times. He gets a laugh out of how dumb I am and drags me along. Guess up there I'll have to stick to Frank Munski – have to have someone to take care of me. Lights out, love, Walter." Walter presents this as a joke but there is truth behind it. He has yet to learn the art of bluffing.

On April 25 he writes, "They say tomorrow, likely in the afternoon, we move. I went to church and that was about all I've done. Went to the show at 1300 & saw 'Happy Go Lucky' in technicolor. "Boy the line some of these boys feed the girls is terrible." Walter is running out of things to say and resorts to calculating how many shaves he can get out of a single razor blade. Finally, he fills the page and closes. "I'll send you my new address soon as I know it. Love, Walter."

Reading has become one of Walter's favorite pastimes. Besides *'Time,'* the *'Saturday Evening Post'* and newspapers, he reads whatever books are available. With the Marines, his reading habit will serve him well as he waits, sometimes for months, for the Marines to plunge into the violent, deadly, combat that their nickname, 'Devil Dogs,' implies.

PART 5 – CAMP PENDLETON – 65 LETTERS
APRIL 27, 1943 – JANUARY 16, 1944

Two days later, April 27, he is writing from Camp Pendleton, about fifty miles north of San Diego. Covering over 120,000 acres, the Marine base is a work in progress. So far, base training facilities include a landing craft school, an amphibious tractor school and a medical field service school. Many of the barracks are without such niceties as hot water showers and beds.

In his letter Walter describes a scene of organized chaos. The corpsmen are assigned to one barracks and moved to another before they can settle in. Walter provides his new address on page one, and the next day crosses it out and provides a second. He has no medical duties and has been chopping and raking weeds. Most of the men are allowed to take leave, but Oceanside, the nearest town, is over nine miles away.

Walter does not mention the circumstances, but "This morning I watched some C.B.s practice embarkation and debarkation from and to those rubber boats out here in the swimming pool. They can really get up some speed …paddling them like a canoe."

He has watched an exhibition baseball game in which Joe DiMaggio struck out, flied out and hit one single. His first night featured a coyote serenade. The next morning, "A grouchy old guy from our group came in with his face all marked up with abrasions. His story was he got off the bus at the wrong place and fell in a ditch – of course we all believe it."

Walter attempts optimism. "I believe I'll like this place if they give me something to do that I like. Did Dad ever get that tobacco pouch and the money order for $100? Maybe you mentioned it in the letter I should have received and may get tomorrow. Love, Walter.

"Camp Pendleton, May 1, Dear Folks, this is Sat & I rate the weekend but I'm staying in. I have 4 letters from you, all unanswered." As Walter moves from place to place throughout the war, his mail will continue to lag behind him. Walter encloses an eight page, 3" by 6" pamphlet, which provides a romanticized history of the area from 1769 to April 1943. This Marine flyer is more amusing than useful.

"You know, I just heard the fellows talking to a fellow down in the squad room who doesn't chew, drink, or smoke. I knew of one other fellow down at Elliott like that.... The fellow who sleeps below me possibly may be the same kind – he doesn't smoke & I'll check & see about the others simply as a point of interest. He's a tough looking customer but may be OK. I've usually found the fellows that are hard to get acquainted with are often the nicest. DeVore has taken a turn for the worse. Since we left, he's been drunk every night & in town most of the time. While I was there... he drank only twice."

Apparently, Myrtle has pressed Walter about the 'gas attack' training he mentioned a few letters ago, because he takes the time to reassure her. "On that gas attack (practice) they used tear gas – real stuff – but of course that's almost harmless."

Walter has received bad news from Mrs. Davis. Her father has died, and her husband's health declines. Walter believes she is "too nervous." He ends with an apology: "I would have liked to have sent candy home but the PX didn't have any boxes for Mother's Day this year- so just sending a card with my Love, Walter."

He sends the card, a flowery one with appropriate verse, in its own envelope. As I look at the envelope, I notice that mail from Pendleton has only one postmark. In Bremerton envelopes were stamped first by the Navy and then later by the USPS, after they arrived in Missoula. The Marines apparently don't bother. Too bad, since now it is impossible to be sure how long letters remain in transit.

When Walter writes on May 5, he has gone a week without any real duties. "Still I've done nothing. I found out for sure my work starts soon, perhaps Monday…. My name is on the list for transfer to the 1st Bn. of the 24th Marines. No doubt we'll stay in this camp. I've heard some of the fellows hoping they would stay with the 24th because they say they are trained to be a crack unit. I don't know anything so don't care where they send me." The machine that will become the 4th Marine Division is gathering personnel, and Walter is swept along. By August, with just over 17,000 men, it will be at full strength.

"Frank Munski is going along with us, and I'm glad. He's a funnier character than Russell Lynn but does have a great deal of sense. He likes good music, reads books from Book of the Month Club etc. He will certainly furnish the morale booster for the company a corpsman is supposed to." For the first time Walter lists 'boosting morale' among a corpsman's duties.

According to Walter's brother David, "Russel Lynn was an old bachelor and lived with his older brother Torrance in an old house on Evaro hill. He went to school with Mother for a few years. He was very slow talking and didn't make much sense a lot of the time. The brothers guarded the Evaro trestle (railroad bridge) against sabotage during WWII. He always carried a big, long barrel pistol. He was a one-of-a-kind character." As to Frank Munski, David recalls that "Walter corresponded with Munski for years after the war and thought well of him."

"Darn the newspapers with their headlines of victory in 1944. They shouldn't disillusion people that way. The Japs are telling their people to prepare for 100 years of war. In a way that is good, for the people won't feel the reverses too hard – and we aren't going to get by too easily." I am impressed by Walter's grasp of the strategic and psychological factors at play. Japan cannot be defeated militarily in 1944, and Americans are impatient. Walter worries that if the war drags on, popular support will wane.

Before closing, Walter remembers to needle Byron just a bit – "… and Byron, have you noticed whether or not the round posts between us & the school section are rotted off yet?"

By May 7 he has no regular duties, and after warning 'The Folks' that, "… this is going to start out strictly as a scuttle butt letter," he speculates. "The rumor seems thick that we may go to the East Coast as the rest of the 24th is over there – likely to New River in N. Carolina. That is Hell they say." While Marines might find this characterization of Camp Lejeune accurate, the rumors have the situation backward. Beginning in early July and continuing into September the main elements of the 4th Division, will leave Lejeune and move west to Camp Pendleton. The entire Division will train as a group there until mid-January 13, 1944, when they will embark from San Diego for the Marshall Islands. In the meantime, and throughout all Walter's service, rumors will remain rampant.

With no duties beyond his training, Walter finds time to describe his new accommodations. They now have hot water and pillows, two mundane but important items previously absent. He has traded his too-large overseas hat for a smaller one. "Soon I'm going (maybe) to send Navy shoes home. I believe Pop can wear them fine."

Although the corpsmen are far from the enemy, they face other hazards. "One of the fellows, & a swell fellow, who came from Elliott with us as a registered pharmacist & PhM2/c, J.D. Miller from Ft. Worth, Texas, was injured badly the other day." It is an old story. Sailor on liberty meets woman with car. Both are drinking, car goes over cliff, law of gravity takes over. Long list of broken body parts follows. Prognosis is poor.

By page four Walter is ready to close. "About time for lights out so I'll send this. Thank David for the letter. It was swell. Soon I'll answer both Byron's & yours. Love Walter. This is a noisy bunch of Marines."

May 11 - As promised, Walter writes a letter to each brother. Byron's has a light almost joking tone even as Walter compares an infestation of crabs to a case of poison oak. His verdict: poison oak is worse. Walter includes a tale about corpsman Deets who was stranded somewhere on the shore of Africa when his ship went down. When he finally caught a ride home, Deets found that he had been passed over for promotion. Walter offers a massive understatement: "Hasn't been lucky about positions for ratings. A good egg though. Think I'll write a note to David. So Long, Walter."

"Dear David, Was I surprised to receive that letter from you!" Again, Walter treats David almost like an adult, cursive writing, and all. "Has Mother got her baby chicks yet? Guess you will have more wood to carry when they start the brooder house fire. Do you see many Sailors and Marines in Missoula? ...I'll bet you pick on Mama now that I'm not there to watch you. I'm going to tell Byron to watch you. Your brother, Walter."

On Monday, May 17, Walter writes again. He has been at Pendleton three weeks and aside from a little weapons training, his duty so far has consisted of moving his gear from one barracks to another. He describes the Marines' "...little 30 caliber carbines. They have shells about the length of a 25-20 and are the same size.... The guns are made by General Motors and have no windage adjustment & they are not sighted up properly, so we had to aim from 10 inches to 6 feet to the left of the target at 200 yards." He spent an afternoon on the firing range, where he "... shot better than the Marine I was with on standing, surprise, and moving targets." He and the other idle corpsmen "... are having troubles now – Boot Marines don't like corpsmen ...& if we hang around the barracks the officers kick."

His two liberties have given him some respite. He has been hitchhiking and this letter describes the ride through the area outside LA and a weekend spent sightseeing. He has no physical complaints, but the waiting and uncertainty are hard. After four and a half pages he writes, "I just went to chow and can't think of a thing to say now." He then thinks of a few things and fills the last page before closing with "Love Walter, finally bought some envelopes in Ocean Side."

On May 19th Walter writes that the corpsmen are trapped in the classic Catch -22 he mentioned two days before. "We've been catching H – from all sides. (Walter's 'H' here is a first for him and perhaps a sign that the language he must hear every day is starting to rub off.) Colonel issued strict orders for all men to stay out of the barracks. The chief said no we had to be where he could find us although he never wants us.

The colonel, and later the major, caught us and made us march from 1400 to 1530. Tomorrow, chief or no chief, we leave."

The corpsmen's main concern, and a topic for constant scuttlebutt, is their next assignment. "Now we can cross Africa off our list, but South America is still a remote possibility. Aleutian Islands likely not." Walter does not mention any of their more likely destinations, such as the Japanese-held Marshal and Mariana islands, or worse yet, Iwo Jima and Okinawa.

Now that Lloyd DeVore has been transferred, Frank Munski has become Walter's closest friend. He can rely on Munski, and in Walter's words, "I get an awful kick out of Frank."

May 23, 1943, Walter has just returned from the hospital in "Dago" where he visited Miller, the corpsman who was badly injured in a car wreck. Walter figures "… he will not see service for about a year." Did this accident perhaps save J.D. Miller of Ft. Worth Texas (the only Texan Walter has described as a 'Swell Fellow') from dying on Saipan or Iwo Jima?

"Boy travel is just as bad by bus as it is by hitch hiking – we had to stand all the way…. I bought a medical dictionary in town for $3.00… it's very popular and I have the '43 edition. It's so nice to study from because it's concise. I'm sending along a money order.

"We went to the zoo again…. Got a good look at the snakes. According to them there are four poisonous snakes in the U.S." After listing the main types – Water Moccasin, Copperhead, Rattlesnake and Coral, Walter helpfully notes, "Many of those rattlers are in San Diego County. They must have at least 50 kinds or varieties." He follows that cheery comment with a detailed description of their overnight field exercise in the hills around the camp, which are, of course, excellent snake habitat.

By May 26, Walter is disgusted with Camp Pendleton's seemingly endless supply problems. "Makes me mad – first I couldn't get envelopes at the PX – got some ashore – and now I'm out of paper & they have none." Even worse, the 60,000-man camp is rife with thieves. "It made me so mad - I'm still mad. Monday, I had to leave in a terrible hurry & I didn't lock up my field scarf … and someone stole it… it is the first piece of clothing I have ever had stolen. Had to be Marines. They have been swiping apples and magazines from under my pillow…. I don't trust many of these fellows." Just four months ago, Walter was at Bremerton where the men looked after each other's possessions. Not so here.

Locals also feel strongly about Marines. "Some of the bar tenders here say they will be glad when these East Coast Marines are dead or at least gone. They are a truly rough bunch – from the slums of New York, Pennsylvania (mine region) and Ohio…. You can tell now why sailors get rides in preference to Marines on the highway."

Walter watches a two-day exercise firing machine guns – probably 50 caliber M2 Browning since they were hitting targets at up to 1,000 yards. "… they used tracer bullets every 5th round. Some fun watching them go." Although Walter is not happy with the character of some Marines, he appreciates their equipment. He is particularly impressed by what may be a 'sound powered' field telephone (one which operates without an electrical power source) and by their assortment of all-wheel drive vehicles used in amphibious landings.

When he has time and is not sick, Walter usually writes about what he has seen. He has been to the zoo and he compares their large brown bear to the farm's workhorses. "That's some bear (Kodiak). He really is enormous…, He's as tall as Maggie & legs as large as Jim's front shoulder (almost). The motor transport group have a monkey chained to their building up here…. Sure wish I could send home some of the ammunition they use here. Boy could we have fun. They do. Love, Walter."

May 30, Walter and Lewis have just returned from liberty in L.A. "Got a swell room in the El Ray Hotel for 75 cents – it was clean and swell bed… We went out to the Ice Capades – got the last 2 seats in the house $2.20 but we had good positions…. Dancing on ice is really beautiful…. All kinds of comics, beautiful girls and one of the most applauded features a simple waltzing done by a heavy-set middle-aged man with a lady to match – called them back 3 times."

I grew up without knowing Walter cared about ice skating. Forty years later, with Mom and his folks dead and the ranch sold, I discovered he did. After he married Lee Masters, they watched the Ice

Capades, the figure skating portion of the Winter Olympics, Holiday on Ice and probably any similar televised programs. Now I know the origin of his fascination.

But the Ice Capades was on Saturday, and Walter and Lewis weren't done. "Sunday, we saw China & High Explosives." About this show Walter says exactly nothing. After 'a heavy-set, middle-aged man with a lady to match' waltzed across the ice and into his heart, Walter does not find 'High Explosives' noteworthy.

I am struck by Walter's choice of Lewis as his companion for this outing. His first mention of Lewis was in his Bremerton letter of January 3 when Walters described Lewis as "… one of the funniest, strangest fellows one will ever meet. He acts to me like inbred – but he's smart at book learning and a pretty nice fellow." I believe Walter, given time, was willing, or even eager, to see the good in others.

Next, Walter reports on the field exercise. "Oh yes, I was sort of worried about that 25-mile forced march because I'm not in condition & wondered if I could keep up to the Marines. I did OK – no blisters & worked 2 hrs. that night immediately after chow fixing up the Marines feet & troubles & then went to the show. I'm almost contemptuous (not quite yet) of the rugged fellows. Will have to see first how I come out on the problem this week. March out 25 or so miles Tues & work - returning Friday."

It is late Sunday night and Walter should be exhausted but "… I haven't run down yet. Funny I got hungry for coffee last week & started drinking it…. Not very often that I drink it but tonight I did." Now I understand his six-page letter.

Walter mentions coming 'home' to the base, catches himself, and admits, "Guess we would call a flat spot in the desert the same if we stayed there a little while." He gives a short financial report - sent home $100, on hand $42, next week will send another $40. Myrtle has kept him up to date on the ranch, so he offers her a few words of encouragement.

He is at the bottom of page six, but still manages to squeeze in a bit more. "Guess maybe I'll answer Mrs. Pope's letter & go to bed. Love, Walter. I thoroughly enjoyed this weekend."

Sunday, June 6, exactly a week after his last letter, Walter announces, "Well I lived through the trip." The 'trip' was a four-day field problem which began with an 18-mile, seven-hour march to a tent camp area. The site had a few buildings – a field kitchen, showers and toilets, and officer's quarters but it appears the men slept on the ground in tents.

This was his first real physical test, and even though he carried as much as the Marines, he managed. Many Marines suffered under their fifty-pound packs and Walter worked until dark "… treating blisters, wounds and cactus spines…. About 4 fellows played out going out. The second day … my hips were sore, but we had to go about 2 mi, to the machine gun range & they seemed to be in an awful hurry. The first burst of tracer bullets started a fire, so the rest of the day was spent fighting fire and … burning a fire trail around it. The boys worked till midnight."

Later Walter writes "I believe the hardest job in the world would be that of Second Lt. in the Marines." He goes on to describe a standard feature of these exercises, the use of raiders, Marines who act as enemy infiltrators, and under cover of darkness, try to slip past the sentries and attack the camp. "The first night the guards caught 4 raiders & sent them back minus their clothes. Thereafter they posted double guards (carrying) pick handles, socks filled with sand, brass knuckles, knives…. Had the raiders attacked I'm sure a fellow could have been killed. The whole camp was very tired at night & no mood for playing, but once up would have been very hard to control."

He notes, "I very much dislike the shows they put on for Marines & that the Marines obviously enjoy…. Don't think I'll attend any more on the base – each time they seem to be worse – dirtier."

Finally, almost as an afterthought, he mentions that the company is expecting a ten-day field problem and then notes, "I never saw such large, numerous blisters in my life. Some feet were raw. Wonder how long before my feet start breaking down (the arches)." He closes with his usual "love, Walter", but adds a postscript - "With Pop's power of attorney, he could turn my war bonds over to David for the specific purpose of education, couldn't he? It would be best to have that taken care of before we move on. That is if I don't come back, he could change them? Walt."

Walter's short letter of June 9 begins with optimism. "I have only 6 months more for my enlistment to be up…. All I've done is inspect the company for athletes' foot and … treat a few cases…. Hardly worth my board." When he signed up, did Walter really think his two year enlistment would be honored? Now, eighteen months later, does he still believe it? He must know he is in the war for the duration.

His brother David is about to turn eight, and Walter asks Myrtle about a gift, before closing with a remark about Mary Todd Lincoln. "Poor woman, I don't believe she was ever truly happy or satisfied. Love, Walter."

Some of Walter's comments are jarring. "Still haven't found a Dago I like. Just for the fun of it I copied off a few names from the watch list – Pasaniti, Paulini, Piccalomini, Schlenker, Salachi, & Nadwczynski. Most of this outfit are Dagoes and Poles." Later he mentions the Zoot Suit riots, repeating the Military view which places the blame on the 'Mex.' Given what he read in the papers at the time how could he think otherwise?

As I read Walter's letters, some of his words make me cringe. Words like Dago, Pollack, Mex, Jew, Jap, and, once, Nigger. All are offensive today, but Walter uses them casually. Many of these words I am sure he heard from Pop. When I was growing up, I never heard him use the N word, but he spoke of Jews and when he mentioned the Japanese, which was seldom, they were sometimes Japs.

His parents were a primary influence on Walter. Myrtle believed in segregation, and Pop spoke of 'using an ax handle' to keep order among the Black and Irish workers at the smelter where he was foreman. Unlike his parents, Walter is out in the world and he is beginning to question things he thought he knew. I remember his comment from his March 21 letter where he described the Cajun, Antoine Tabor and wrote "He has lived quite a life. Doesn't seem possible that there are so many parts to the U.S.A." When Walter uses racist words, I believe it is out of ignorance, not malice.

I also believe words must be understood in their historical context. Even before the attack on Pearl Harbor, both Japan and the United

States were imperial powers with conflicting interests. Once World War Two began, racism on both sides grew ever uglier. Fueled by movies and other propaganda, it quickly became a battle between 'Dirty Japs' and 'Yankee Dogs.' So it goes.

Walter does not write again till June 19. This nine day gap between his letters is the longest so far. He will continue to write regularly, but there will be times when he is at sea or in combat, when over three weeks will pass between his letters.

On June 19 he writes, "… well they tried to kill us but didn't quite succeed." The field exercise lasted five days, the packs weighed 75 pounds, and at 2130 on Monday, after a ten-mile march, the men started cross-country. "They had to lower the carts into ravines & lift them out, climb innumerable mountains and hills. We lost several men on the way from exhaustion, one from raw heel, and arrived here at 0445 wet and cold." Their rations, he informs his parents, "… were 3 egg sandwiches, and always on a march or problem, regardless of length, we have had only one qt of water to drink."

Walter has made his point and could stop there but he presses on for another page, throwing in an overnight exercise, complete with artillery and lightning. Walter marches the same miles and carries the same weight as the Marines. After he works into the night treating their injuries, Walter writes, "In spite of my hearty dislike for the Marine Corps & Marines in general, I like some of these fellows very much."

"June 27, Camp Pendleton. Guess it's about time to write again. Its 1800 & I'm back from 3 days in L.A.… saw The Camel Caravan, with Bing Crosby… 3 very good negro tap dancers, a very good piano team … certainly got an ovation." The comics were not so good: "The jokes were about the same one hears at Marine gatherings and vulgar." With no explanation, Walter switches to 'negro' certainly an acceptable term in 1943, and he never uses the term 'nigger' again in his letters. Perhaps someone told him it was an offensive word.

"I told you this was a good group of corpsmen – finally we have been officially recognized… We were individually praised and as a group we have been given a few privileges such as being paid ahead of the Marines instead of very last."

As to the money he has been sending home, "I'm satisfied that you are going to use the money for something else than bonds.... Would rather have cash or preferably machinery." This is the second time Walter has questioned the value of war bonds as an investment.

Walter and Frank Munski think California is a wonderful state, "... but we both agree that Montana or Idaho is where we want to be." Walter ventures north to Pasadena, and later visits the Capistrano Mission to the south. He hitchhikes or rides a bus. As he learns the area, travel becomes routine. "Funny to me that I can run around & get back – a year or so ago that would have been impossible for me. Love, Walter."

In his June 30th letter he opens, "Now I have 3 letters to answer of yours.... So glad in a way to hear you have sold the sheep. Wonder how hard it will be to get started again.... Nice to be rid of Burge, (a notoriously lazy Chief) the work is still coming back that should have been taken care of three months ago.... There is no doubt in my mind now that Sgt Zercawski is mentally unbalanced. Never did like him – other corpsmen agree with me.... Nothing interesting to say so - Love, Walter."

July 4 - "This has seemed the least like a 4th of any I've ever spent." Back home, July Fourth gatherings were special as relatives of all ages gathered at the ranch for a massive family picnic, and Myrtle reigned by the force of her personality. Camp Pendleton is an alien place. Walter is isolated, and Munski is probably the only corpsman he would call a friend.

To make the best of it, Walter takes liberty and visits the Davis'. "Each time I go to the Davis' place I'm reminded of their wealth.... They have all sorts of things that are very expensive, but not showy." Still, their material opulence can only remind him of Al and Myrtle's situation on the ranch. Perhaps that is why he writes, "I've got quite a bit of extra money on hand & I'll send it home.... My but it would have come in awful handy at times a few years ago."

Before he closes, Walter alludes to wartime censorship rules. "Sometime we'll have to work out a code so you can get an idea where I'm at when I shove off?? Love, Walter."

July 6 marks the start of what will be a full month spent at Tent Camp #2. "Dear Folks, Gotcher letter today & guess I'll write a note now." 'Gotcher'? Really, Walter, have you forgotten Miss Helen Fink and Senior English? Perhaps, but to be fair, he is tent camping in the desert in July, and although he takes liberty some weekends, he also joins the Marines on their day-long marches and strenuous training exercises. He does this while treating the Marines for sunburn, poison oak and eye infections. He has learned some short cuts. For example, on the obstacle course, "When they crawled thru the fence I went around & poured on the iodine – didn't bother about crawling through."

Whatever literary problems Walter may have he does not suffer from writer's block. This July his eight letters to the 'Folks' will fill twenty-one pages. This is above average, even for Walter.

"We have an NCO meeting tonight so guess I'll have to attend. So far never gone to one.... Munski & many more made 2/c. I probably could have made 1/c because they gave no tests, but I told them I wasn't ready. Having a terrible time with Company tonight. Guess they need more work. Love, Walter."

Walter claims not to be 'ready,' but he has studied and knows the material. In the view of other corpsmen and several doctors, he knows his job and does it well. Giving orders remains difficult for him.

July 10, from Tent Camp 2 he writes, "This is Saturday evening and I'm pretty well satisfied. Rode into the base and got a Post, some candy, shaving soap and a flashlight." He has straightened up his area, his laundry is soaking, and he has time to write. The 23rd Marines have arrived and the 25th is expected soon. The 4th Marine Division is forming, and Walter doesn't expect they will leave Pendleton till November. Their exercises, or as Walter calls them, 'our problems,' keep coming and he has begun to actually enjoy them. Referring to the 'blank cartridges' they were issued he remarks, "Boy was that fun to pop at a fellow when he showed up…. It was the first time I've enjoyed a problem…. Think I'll read the Post till dark… Love, Walter."

July 15th – After ten days at Tent Camp 2 there is a mail delivery, and Walter receives five letters from five different folks. While he waits for patients to trickle in, he sits down to reply. "Dear Folks, …. Lots of scuttlebutt which the Marines seem to thrive on. The Major and 3 or 4 other officers have been restricted to their tents for a few days because they went down to San (illegible) & met their wives…. We haven't done anything since we've been out & these Marines don't get along that way very good because they are restless & noisy – complaining & insubordinate." Walter has changed his mind about promotion. "Really I would much prefer to stay here with my Co. because we get along swell but if I'm ever going to make 1/c I'm going to learn at least most of what I need before I make it."

Marines continue to arrive from various locations, mostly Camp Lejeune, and "You can bet the sick bay is in an uproar. The Chief turned in with Malaria, Ferris may be transferred & Blevins, the best man we've had, is trying for a transfer."

"Had to take a Cheatgrass seed out of the mascot's eye (MacTavish). Kind of hard to work on but it turned out OK & makes the Gunny – Gunnery Sgt – feel very good." Walter knows about Cheatgrass from home. An invasive weed, it is an ideal fuel for range fires. Cheatgrass has sharp, barbed seeds which pierce skin and enter eyes, ears, and mouths of animals. The seeds are hard to remove and can cause serious harm.

"PX truck came out yesterday, first time in a week…. They sold out fast because nearly everyone was out of smokes & candy…. Getting Dark – 2015 – Love, Walter."

July 19, based on Walter's comments, stress is high, and discipline is an ongoing problem - "Ferris is out of the brig. He & the Chief stole alcohol from sick bay & went on unauthorized liberty." A Marine major – "J.V.V. Veeder (Dutch, 6'7" tall) implies he's been in Guad (Guadalcanal) etc. but actually he cracked up before getting there." I expect Walter knows a lie when he hears one – by now he has certainly heard plenty.

Tent Camp #2 July 21st – Walter is now in Hq Co. (headquarters company) and working as the second in charge at sick call. He is a bit worried because "… Grady isn't around much. He really knows his medicine – nice to have him around to talk to & consult. Knows more than the Drs about some kinds and uses."

Everyone is on edge. "Dr Shiring is back from field Med school … he & Dr Okulicy are hardly on speaking terms. We'll have to be very careful or we'll wind up on one or the other's black list."

Now that he is around more men who have seen combat, Walter is hearing more and more 'war stories,' some of them quite graphic. For some reason he shares one in a letter. I wonder if he considers how it might affect his parents.

Walter wonders about the food. "Funny how they feed here. In 'D' Co. the boys don't get enough to eat & poor quality such as cold or no meat, no butter and such. Up here in Hq. Co. get good steaks, roasts, plenty of jam & bread. Certainly is something wrong somewhere." Walter must realize Headquarters Company is fed better deliberately. He is now 168 pounds, up 20 from his enlistment.

The 4th is an entirely new division, created piecemeal from raw recruits and parts stripped from other divisions. If the commandant of an existing division is required to give up a portion of his force, is he likely to send his best or someone like the PhM2c who "… turned in to the Hosp. with imaginary troubles trying for limited service in his record – so many fellows are trying & some are getting away from this outfit."

Late afternoon, July 25th and Walter has spent nearly three weeks, with occasional breaks, at Tent Camp 2. "Dear Folks, Sunday & a letter waiting here. I went down to Dago as we had Friday, Sat & Sun off & I looked up DeVore. He is the same as ever – wrote me out a special chow pass and liberty card so that I could ride home with him on the married man's bus."

The world may shift on its axis but DeVore is constant. He still cuts corners, slips through loopholes, and blusters his way through the world. A little harmless forgery appears to be all in a day's work. Walter sometimes yearns to be more like DeVore.

"He (DeVore) and his wife live out at Ocean Beach in a small shack.... $40 per mo. He has a very nice wife – a Swede that's about 5'10 1/2" & a couple years older than he. She is immaculate in habits & house cleaning.... We all went up to La Fiesta Café & had a swell chicken dinner. Served baked potatoes which was very nice. The best thing about the place was the cleanliness & plenty of light & no flies which is extraordinary around here. I can hardly write now because of the deer flies."

The Marines will be at Tent Camp a bit longer, "... because on their last problem the communications got fouled up." Walter's problems, though, are with the weather and a grass fire burning near camp. "Gee it's hot here now. I really suffer, it's as bad as 100F at home.

"Gee they have some bum Doctors at the Dispensary. Tonsillectomies take 5-7 days before they can eat. Byron was OK in about 3 as I remember.... Love, Walter."

July 28th – "Dear Folks, well now we are back in camp, away back in. We moved into the 16 area which is about 2 ½ miles from our old place but the barracks are new and pretty good – a very noticeable shortage of metal though. No door knobs or metal fixtures and the studding still shows – not finished inside. We had the sick bay set up ready for operation in about 1 hour after the truck stopped."

Walter writes in a stream-of -consciousness or scatter-gun style. He darts from topic to topic and covers a wide area. "If I ever get home, I could tell you some stories about how tough the Marines really acted – feeding Japs to crocodiles etc..... Fellow is trying to sell new Navy shoes 6 ½ for $2.... I flunked my swimming test again, next time I believe I'll cheat & put my name on the list.... I'll finish this tomorrow. They are bothering me too much.... Ensign Burge has been reported 'over the hill' since last Friday.... Twenty some years in service & now he runs the risk of being broken to seaman if he can't explain it... a fellow used carbolic acid for poison oak, burns all over his body.... Gibson talked about going into opium den. Took one puff..."

These are mad, desperate times. While Marines talk of atrocities, one man smears his body with acid, and another becomes a deserter. Gibson dabbles in drugs, and Walter? Walter contemplates falsifying Marine records to show he has passed the swimming test. Where will it end?

July 31 – "Dear Folks, I'm writing a day early so that tomorrow I can get ready for the field…. At 0645 we fall out with heavy transport packs and leave for the week." A heavy transport pack was 70 to 75 pounds.

"Yesterday was a busy one for me. We had a large sick call and had to examine about 30 – 35 fellows for mess duty. I picked up one that they had passed – he had trench mouth…. I gave the fellow 1 cc of Bismuth subsalicylate…. A long needle is used, and it is pushed – fast – into the gluteus maximus muscle. He said he didn't feel it so I guess I must have done O.K. Dr Okulicy watched."

It would have pleased Walter immensely to catch a problem missed by a doctor and then be able to administer treatment himself. He then gives detailed physical descriptions of the two doctors who have been feuding for some time. Walter gets along best with Okulicy, "…a heavy featured, slow speaking, quiet almost sullen Polack." Shiring is good looking, but "… an ear-banger and very absent minded. When we consult him if he doesn't know just what to do, he walks off & starts to do something else…. May not write till next Sunday. Love, Walter."

On Saturday, August 7th, back from a week-long field problem, Walter is in the dumps. "We got all messed up on our problem & med corps wasn't complimented either… Felt fine & started caring for some fellows without my helmet on & all at once I fell out with heat stroke - sick for a couple days, diarrhea, headache etc." Perhaps Walter would have been fine but for the Marines 'one quart of water per day' policy.

"Had a terrible day yesterday. Still didn't feel very well & I broke my watch & locked my keys to my locker box inside." His only good news is the arrival of his camera, and for that he is happy.

They are scheduled for another field problem. "Said it's going to be the toughest terrain hit so far – must be terrible. I've got our medical unit packed. They always leave that up to me. Makes me mad at times. I get the blame for everything that goes wrong.

"I owe everyone a letter now but guess they'll have to wait till I get around to them. Darn but I miss my watch. At first, I didn't like the thing but lately I got very attached to it. Love, Walter."

On Saturday, August 14, the large regimental problem is over, and Walter's mood is upbeat. The exercise featured infantry, artillery, amphibious tractors, and air support. Walter wasn't bothered by the heat this time, and besides treating the usual blisters and sunburn, he "pulled cactus spines out of a fellow's tongue." With that, Walter describes the taste of the cactus seed pods as "… raspberry & a cross with watermelon.

"Guess I'll go take a shower – boy they're nice. I was too tired to go on week end. Had planned to watch Kendrick get married… but has to wait a week. He wants me to be best man but I'm afraid I wouldn't be of any help…. Love, Walter."

A week passes and Walter does not write. Finally, on August 23, he manages, "Bet you thought I've been shipped out. This will be short – feel pretty good because of a nice weekend - & I'm trying to hold down 2 jobs…. I go up to the Dispensary after I finish sick call & help Grady in the pharmacy just for fun."

Walter's promise to be Kendrick's best man turned into a saga. "Missed the cab leaving camp so had to take overcrowded liberty bus – driver said 'No more' but …climbed on before he shut the door… got into LA & hitchhiked – rode a motorcycle double part way. Got to PE station 1 hr. late at 1800 … ran into Kendrick on the street & he had a room for me. Then at 2030 I acted as best man at his wedding at First Baptist Church. Just 4 guests…. They had candles for light in a small reception room & had cake & coffee there. Sunday, I attended church there. Large crowd friendly people & very nice minister, also nice church."

I can't imagine the Walter of a year before managing such a journey alone. DeVore and Munski would be proud. After describing his eventful weekend, Walter closes with an understatement I find hilarious. "Don't be surprised if I miss letters – sort of hard writing them when nothing going on. Love, Walter."

"August 25, Dear Folks, Gee, it scared me when I read about Pop. Surely good you could get to the hospital like that. It would be very good to have some aromatic spirits of ammonia in the house."

If all I had was this letter, I would be at a loss. I never heard the rest of this story from Pop or Myrtle, and according to Walter's second-hand version, Pop was stung by a bee (or bees?) and suffered a severe reaction. Myrtle feared for his life and drove him to the hospital.

This version contradicts the well-known fact that Myrtle did not, would not, could not, drive. Except, this one time, she did. It was a miracle, if you will, and deserves more fanfare than Walter allows. Myrtle could do most anything. She could drive a team of horses, birth lambs, butcher turkeys and shoot a bear. Her nemesis was the 'dad-blamed infernal combustion engine.' Nevertheless, an hour or so after Pop was stung, she had him in the hospital twelve miles away.

Fortunately, we have another witness. David would have been eight in 1943 and as he remembers it there were actually two incidents. In the first, "They were papering the front room of the old house, when a wasp stung Pop while he was on the ladder." As David tells it, Pop barely made if off the ladder before fainting and Byron drove hm to the hospital where he received a shot of adrenaline. Later that summer, Pop got stung again, but this time, David says, "Byron was not at home... so Mother who had never driven got him in the car and took him to a neighbor's place." Eventually she found someone to take him into the hospital in Missoula where he was treated.

Back at Pendleton, Walter and his fellow Guinea pigs are testing army gas masks in a chamber filled with Lewisite, a toxic gas, soon to be abandoned by the US military because it isn't toxic *enough*. Poison gas might prove a nuisance, but Walter's real concern is his inability to pass the Navy's mandatory swimming test. Walter prepares to 'fix' Navy records to show his compliance. Afterwards, did he light a candle to De-Vore and Munski, the patron saints of loop holes and fudged paperwork?

It is August 29, and as new Marines arrive, Walter is performing examinations. "Never supposed that men in the physical condition that some of these men are, would ever be transferred to a combat outfit.

Some of them need surgery right now. Also, we found 10 cases of crab lice.... Yesterday I saw a new case. It was diagnosed as shingles." One of the corpsmen, Cochrane, is no help. "I never saw anyone who was so lazy and felt less guilty about it. I suppose his folks had Negro servants to help him in the house etc."

Walter mentions a more serious problem. "One thing I am going to have to get straight is this matter of some of the fellows using the narcotics. Guess maybe we'll get a lock box and put the stuff in it and give the key to the doctor because I can hardly refuse to give the key to the chief when he asks for it. At first, I thought it was shell shock... but now I know it is whiskey and narcotics. Before he gives a first aid lecture ... he takes a shot or a drink."

Walter writes, "The news looks very good from Europe now. What they need is a revolution to help the Allies to get a foothold on the continent proper." Walter closes after a review of The Robe, an inspirational, semi-historical novel set in the time of Jesus. He tells Myrtle, "It's a very good story, sometimes the way it's narrated is tiresome, but the plot and story are really tops. Wish you could get it to read." Walter may have sent Myrtle a copy. – I remember being on the ranch in the late 1950s and finding a red cloth-bound copy of Lloyd C. Douglas's 600 page doorstop on a bookshelf in Myrtle's living room. Like Walter, I found portions of Douglas's narrative 'tiresome'.

On September 1, as Marines continue to pour in from Camp Lejeune via the Panama Canal, Walter writes, "Time for chow but will wait till the others get back. We had a real sick call this AM – 56 and there will be more in at 1300. Mostly these new fellows with colds.... Trying to make appointments for 7 or 8 for tonsillectomy today.... Guess I'd better clean up this place now. Sick call over again, but another big one this evening for crabs & athletes' feet."

Walter has been without a watch for three weeks, and though he now has a replacement, the constant rumors are disorienting. He admits that the stress is affecting him, writing, "I'm so darned nervous the past couple weeks it's terrible. Lost about 15 pounds, guess the Marine Corps is getting me.... Two men were transferred this A.M. According to Blevins my name is at the top of the list of 2/c that the Dr wants to keep. Possibly they will get better duty than we have but I'd rather stay – at least for a while. I've got a ticket to L.A. for the weekend. Maybe I'll feel more satisfied if I get away from the base for a while.... Love, Walter."

In a post script, Walter airs his worries about Pop. "Funny that bees should effect Pop after all these years of being stung – must be something he could do."

Monday morning, September 6, after his weekend liberty, Walter writes again. He was on the bus to L.A. Friday night when it overheated, so he hitchhiked, something which has become routine for him. The next morning he ventured back to Pershing Square and took a look at the Biltmore Hotel.

"Of course, it's too expensive – I think – for me to ever want to stop there. You should see the service & the rooms, ice water piped to the rooms, all kinds of room service, 4 elevators running all the time.... Something much better, I found a place to eat. Clifton's Cafeteria is very beautiful, very picturesque... a person can get all he can eat for $1. My meals came to 33 cents once & 77 cents the next time. They are a religious group & ...if you wish the meal is free... entertainers singing Old Rugged Cross...If you ever come to L.A. never miss this place." Clifton's was a Los Angles institution; founded in 1935 it expanded to seven different locations. It was hard to describe – a sort of neon, jungle-themed -Tiki Bar with hymn-singing Christian hospitality. It still operates today from a single site.

Back from liberty, Walter is rejuvenated. The break has helped, and his problems are ordinary. His pay has been delayed, money he has loaned out is slow coming back, and this morning's breakfast was 'no good.' But these are problems he can handle, and as he writes, "I've got this sick bay running pretty well. I haven't run out of anything for a while and I have all my reports filed."

Even so, Walter "Would like to ... do something else. I get so tired of the Marine Corps at times I don't know what to do. Next week we start out on another problem. We will undoubtedly have our hands more than full with these new fellows. Certainly a bunch of gold bricks & physically unfit men in this group. Guess their mentality is about average for a Marine. Don't buy any more bonds with my money ... Love, Walter."

On Wednesday, September 9, just three days after reporting how well things were going, Walter begins his next letter with a disclaimer. "The condition I'm in I know I shouldn't write a letter but here goes. Everything has gone wrong today. A whole bunch of men to examine and the health records are messed up.... Also today I made my first mistake and boy was it one. Lt. Reynolds has me on his list and underscored."

So, Walter is on the lieutenant's S--- list. He must have done something really bad – maybe wrecked a jeep or committed some horrible medical mistake that resulted in injury or worse. Perhaps he faces a court martial? Well, no. His great sin? He sent a handful of men to sick bay in the wrong order. Leave it to a Marine colonel to turn a molehill into a mountain. Walter continues, "The battalion heard about it all the way up to the colonel.... Dr. Shiring stood up for me though and said to think nothing more of it."

Walter is not comforted and instead imagines something else that will reflect badly on him. "We are having a terrible time trying to get supplies for the sick bay and I'm running short – that will be the next thing the doctor will have to holler about." I imagine DeVore in Walter's place. I can hear him bluster and bluff his way through the situation. But Walter is conscientious, a perfectionist, sensitive to every mistake, especially the public ones.

His confession over, Walter pretends an interest in events back home, but his heart is not in it and he closes with, "*&%$# I'm getting out of here because as long as I'm around they leave the work for me to do – just transferred two more men to the disp. We're getting rid of them almost as fast as we get them – terrible shape. Goodnight, Walter." Walter almost never closes a letter without sending his love.

September 12, three days later, Walter writes again, and rehashes his mistake and humiliation in painful detail, concluding, "All in all it was one terrible day." As bad as this day was for Walter, no one around him was shot, blown up, drowned, or bayonetted. That, of course, will change.

He continues, "Tomorrow at 0700 we fall out to go on amphibious landings which are scheduled to last all day…. Then we have to make some landings at 0200… work long hours and very little sleep."

The rest of the letter is misery-free and describes Walter's daily activities. "Guess I'd better get my pack ready for our trip, also have another letter to write to Lloyd and Lena. Love, Walter."

September 17, 1943. It has become obvious to Walter that he will be deployed with the 4 Marine Division in the Pacific. The Division was formally activated at Camp Pendleton on August 16, and men have continued to pour into the camp. As of today, the Division is at full strength with 17,831 men. The quality of the men is another matter. Walter has already described some as "…gold bricks, physically unfit and lazy."

Supplies and equipment are crated for transit and amphibious exercises take place weekly. He writes, "Tuesday we … boarded the barges at 0300 … and took off up the coast…. I got pretty sick." Later in the exercise, "I got just a little sick…. A couple more trips & I don't believe I'd get sick."

Back in the dispensary, Walter writes, "We are having trouble with … the fellows drinking the *(medicinal)* alcohol so we put ipecac in it. If they drink enough… they will heave their toenails."

The doctor is trying to give the new HA2/c, some on the job training, and Walter writes, "They certainly don't know much yet. I guess I'm still in charge, but he told me to let another fellow write names & for me to supervise. Don't know if it's a demotion or a promotion." With this unexpected spare time, Walter decides to "…keep track of all men we transfer to dispensary or hospital & when they are discharged. So far that has never been done." Walter regularly is asked where individual men are and this way, he hopes to have answers.

"Am sending 40 – will keep 5 just in case - must have over 100 either loaned out or on hand. Would rather have it in bank. Love, Walter."

Walter's letter of September 20, a Monday, comes after he spent the weekend with Kendrick in Long Beach. Included with his letter is the First Methodist Church bulletin. "Went to the Methodist Church

Sunday. Certainly enjoyed the sermon…. He asked what w
happened if the Good Samaritan had come along at the time or the
beating – what would he have done? He says the church has to stand
behind the war once it is declared…. didn't leave Long Beach till 0300
and arrived at the barracks … ate chow and started on sick call."

Walter has more responsibility now. "Nobody around here now to
keep the boys in line since Blevins is gone. They sort of leave it up to
me and I certainly dislike the job. Sort of have to do it though, being
senior 2/c and no 1/c present." Like it or not, Walter seems to be doing
a good job. "Everything went very smooth today being Monday and all.
We had about 60 men for sick call today… and one examined for the
Brig. Seems that we are getting at least one every day now. The major
from D company is driving some of his men to it and some of the rest
are just getting tired – we need a transfer I guess." Perhaps Walter is
implying that the major needs to be transferred.

The colonel insists that shirts must be starched, a real pain, and Walter
has been ironing his instead, so far with success. "Guess that's about all
for now. Love." Walter forgets to sign, a rare lapse.

September 23, worn down by the volume of work, Walter writes,
"Dear Folks, something is wrong – I'm working too hard. Somehow,
I've got to make more fellows responsible for certain jobs. Kendrick was
transferred yesterday … He was a brass front for me – too much at times.
I'd try to keep him calmed down." Walter has used 'brass' to describe
DeVore and Munski, and in this context it seems to refer to the ability
to dominate others through speech and force of personality. Walter has
the medical skills and knowledge, but 'brass' is all but impossible.

Walter needs to delegate many of his duties, but that would require
him to confront the other, less senior corpsmen. He finds that so dis-
tasteful that, "I've almost decided to put in for submarine duty. I would
get … schooling and then the duty would be better. Couldn't be worse.
We would be in clean surroundings & wouldn't be out in the Malaria
infested hills. It wouldn't be any more dangerous." Only some of Walter's
statements are accurate. Malaria vectors are indeed present in Southern
California, and eradication efforts with DDT are ongoing. But 'clean

surroundings' in a claustrophobia inducing submarine in 1943? Diesel fumes, sweat, hydraulic fluid, sewage and cooking odors, all in a confined space, would form a nauseating miasma. For Walter to even consider submarine duty, his life at Pendleton must feel almost intolerable.

One main reason for his discontent is the commander of D company, which "… is certainly going to the dogs since the new Major took over. They really hate him…Men are deserting the company almost daily. 2 sgts & 2cpls left yesterday…. 2 corpsmen from the company said they were going over the hill tomorrow night, but I think it's just talk." Walter goes on like this for almost four pages and closes with an assessment – "I'm not learning anything here anymore…. Love, Walter."

Walter's next letter typed and dated "September 26, 1943," is on internal Marine communication stationary. "Dear Folks, started this out for Grady as a letter to the bureau and made a mistype so had to start over … no use to waste the paper so decided to write to you….

"Saturday, we had a regimental parade …. It lasted about 1 hour …but of course we were standing around 1 ½ hours preparing for the thing. We were presented with a flag whatever significance that has…. We had to hold a hand salute while they fired a 21-gun salute. It made our arms so tired that they were stiff." The more Walter sees of Marine pomp and ceremony, the more obvious his cynicism.

Walter touches briefly on other subjects, "Monday 2 corpsmen and the chief will probably be transferred because of their active cases of malaria…. fired the carbines again. I didn't do as well as I did the first time. Even with that I made a better score than the Marine I was firing with." The rifles always pull to the left, which annoys Walter. "Can't see the sense of having a rifle that doesn't hit what you are aiming at.

"We are sending some of the new fellows to the hospital as psycho cases now for observation and survey…. Rather interesting observing the actions of these fellows and seeing what the doctors think of them also."

Walter makes one comment related to the ranch. "It would be nice to have the Dunkleberg place but I'm afraid I haven't money enough at home to pay for it. How much do you think it would be worth? Not over $400 is it. Probably the taxes and mortgage would amount to more than that."

Tuesday, 2105 hours, September 28, he writes, "I've just finished packing my pack & the sick call unit. Tomorrow we're scheduled to fall out previous to 0800 & start our hike – 17 miles of very rough ground with heavy transport packs. The 3rd Bn. Went out last week & 30 odd men fell out on one hill – over 100 have been sent back we hear. We're going up into the Santa Margarita Range."

The Margaritas are just north of Camp Pendleton, and although the highest point is only 3,100,' the terrain is brutal for men carrying 70-pound transport packs. Walter will be the senior corpsman. At least he has been able to scrounge some basic items – tape, Merthiolate, benzoin etc.

With the Battalion's two-week problem a night away, Walter writes, "Today I ran a complete physical on a fellow for shipping out. Always before the chief had done that. Fun to use some of the instruments again…. I'll be okay even if I don't write. Love, Walter."

By October 6, the men have been at Tent Camp 3 for a week. The field exercise is half over, and Walter tries to sound modest. "They say it's 37 miles by road back to camp. We came to the foot of a hill 1 ½ miles long & ¾ of a mile high the first day, and the second we climbed it & went on into Casey Springs…. They are getting rather easy." Then, lest anyone think the 45 degree slope was really easy, he adds, "When the Third Bn. went on this problem 38 men fell out from exhaustion on the hill."

The exercise was uneventful except for "Terrible chow…110 in the shade… & dozens coming into sick bay for poison oak…. The other day I thought I had lots to tell you but now it's just tiresome procedure. Love, Walter."

By Sunday morning, October 10, the exercise has three days to run, and Walter remains busy treating poison oak cases. It is still hot, and the food has not improved. Walter is so bored he listens to part of the Catholic mass, though he writes, "…. Couldn't understand anything…. Dr. Shiring has a radio, so today we'll listen to the world series.

"I can't understand why none of our men have been bitten by a snake yet. On one of the field problems, some snakes crawled into the gun emplacements & chased the men out."

Walter makes a statement that may have confused Myrtle. "As for fixing up my room for me, it doesn't matter because my next leave will be for 30 days no doubt." Apparently, Myrtle expects that Walter will be granted sufficient leave to allow him to come home before he ships out and wants to 'fix up his room.' This seems like a normal maternal urge, yet Walter says it doesn't matter. He will not clarify this statement for two weeks.

Walter warns Myrtle to expect delays in overseas mail service. "Mom as soon as I am shipped out there is no point in writing any oftener than every 10 days because it usually takes mail from 1 to 2 months to catch up with one." After averaging two letters a week from her son for almost two years, this will be a big change.

Walter closes, as he often does, with an abrupt subject change. "It looked just now like a plane crashed & pilot jumped. They took the ambulance & went to see…. Guess that's all for now. Love, Walter."

When Walter writes again on October 14, it is from a Los Angles hotel room he is sharing with Munski and Baker. They plan to relax, try to find some decent chow, take in a movie, and maybe go bowling. While Munski runs an errand, Walter describes their last exercise which ended with a forced march. "We marched in Monday night starting at 2200 and made the 28 miles (as measured by our ambulance jeep) in 9 hrs. & 7 minutes…. My tendons in the back of my knees are still sore. 56 men fell out as compared with over 100 in the 3rd Bn & we made it 1 hr. & 15 minutes faster."

Besides Dr. Shiring, a new man, Dr. Porter, is now with the Bn and Walter gives both passing marks. "I like Dr. Porter more all of the time. He's very considerate and slow acting but he's consistent. Dr. Shirling made full Lt the other day too. Nice to see him get it."

When Munski returns the three men eat and go bowling. Later they watch "For *Whom the Bell Tolls,* which Walter describes as "… a swell picture in technicolor & lots of emotion of all kinds so can understand why they rate it high." Walter then surprises me by adding something Myrtle surely wouldn't approve. "Baker picked up a ------ & took her out. I intend to get some sleep tonight and see the play tomorrow.... Bought a new Post so will read a while. Love, Walter."

"October 17, Dear Folks, this seems so much like Monday I can hardly keep straight." Sunday or Monday, what does it matter? Walter belongs to the Marines and, to paraphrase John Prine, 'the days just repeat themselves like some forgotten dream that they've just seen.' Walter continues with a burst of remarks. "Three fellows overdue... my watch stopped in the field, probably corrosion...Lt. injured arm in auto accident, amputated...heard of train wreck in Billings...didn't get to see 'The Drunkard' couldn't get reservations...rode the San Diegan, a streamlined train, very nice... Mom, could you send me silk thread, want it for suturing."

Walter seems resigned, and in less than three months he will ship out. For the past month he has been running roll after roll of film through his camera. He plans to send the pictures home. He never mentions it, but 'if the worst happens' – the unspeakable – at least those images would survive.

October 20, Walter states, "I have no letter to answer from you but it's writing day, so I'll start. Nothing of importance has happened since last time." Walter's next statement contradicts this. With supplies always short, "Grady & I are building up a reserve stock of some hard to get & essential drugs for the shoving off day – opium, acids, suture material, anesthetics etc..... Dr. Shiring has turned in to the hospital with Otitis Media – sure hope we don't lose him." Occasionally Walter drops a few Latin terms, and I wonder, will Byron have to check to discover Dr. Shiring is suffering from an ear ache?

Walter explains why he refused a possible transfer to another outfit. "Kendrick offered me a chance to apply for duty with his outfit because they need more men.... I didn't take it because I didn't want to work with him.... He has picked me out & even though it sort of flatters me, I can't like him." It is interesting, Walter can work with almost anyone, but, given a choice, he quickly becomes particular.

121

He remains very averse to conflict, even with a man like Raley, who is frequently late returning from leave. Walter writes, "Something drastic is going to have to be done with Raley – hope it isn't me that has to do it. Love, Walter."

Just three days later, October 23, Walter writes another long, and in places, disturbing letter. His uncertainty and worry are obvious. "Guess I told you *(he hasn't)* we board ship & make landings against the 2 Bn & then vice versa."

Walter is still toying with the idea of becoming a submariner. "I have the form letter for submarine duty but have to take a physical & look up some of the references." Myrtle has apparently asked why. "I believe things there wouldn't be so muddled up as here. I'm almost afraid to go out with the stuff – equipment & medicines we have on hand. The things we use the most of I don't believe would last two weeks in battle."

As deployment nears Walter bemoans some of the loans he has made. "I know one thing I'm going to stop loaning out money. I've lost $10 on the Chief and Kendricks still has $15. They will pay if.

"These men act just like children, never do anything until told by an officer or NCO. All men regardless of age or ability are treated almost as children until they become sergeants. Guess that's the service though."

Walter closes with a final request, "I may want you to try to get me some surgical instruments later if I can't get them here. Love, Walter."

Among Walter's October letters, there is an envelope addressed to his brother, Byron. Postmarked October 24, the card would have arrived about a week before Byron turned 20. Inside, below the uninspired rhyming verses (Date/Celebrate and Hand/Command) Walter has written, "With Best Wishes, Walter." The front of the card is decorated by a generic bouquet of pink and blue flowers. In an inexplicably bizarre touch, a crescent shaped piece of sandpaper, perhaps 60 grit, has been glued to the base of the bouquet. The sandpaper does not appear to be a retrofit, so perhaps Walter didn't have a lot of choices.

Over a period of four days, October 26 thru 29, Walter writes four pages. "Dear Folks, have some time to spare tonight so will write awhile…. Went out Sunday & Monday returning 1700 Monday." During this overnight problem, "I passed out about 20 aspirin & packed the Sgt. Major's nose with ephedrine. A waste of time for 28 corpsmen & 1 doctor. Should have had 1 doctor & 2 corpsmen.

"I like Dr. Porter more all of the time. He hates the Marine Corps as much as we do & isn't afraid to say so…. Today our definite date was set for sailing. From several points of view looks like straight dope this time." In September Walter speculated that they would ship out very early in January. Now he does not give a date but says "… it will be about 1 month earlier than my second guess."

Myrtle has been assuming that she would see her son before he is deployed. Some passages in his letters were ambiguous on this point but now Walter, still writing on the 26th, tells her emphatically that she will not. "I thought you understood by that remark my 30-day leave meant I wasn't coming home until I come back from overseas. That's the only time they're granted & not always then." For some unknown reason, Walter holds on to the letter till the 29th when he adds a final page.

If Walter had posted the letter October 26, it would have arrived in Missoula toward the beginning of the next week. This would have been crushing news for Myrtle, but in a twist of fate that is never explained, Walter was granted a one week leave. After a long train ride, he arrived at the ranch November 2, perhaps the same day as his letter. No written record of his visit exists, but I checked with his younger brother, David, who remembers, "He picked me up at school, probably on Tuesday, so he probably didn't know about the leave till Sunday, and he had no way to contact the folks."

Walter's next letter is written from the Lakershim Hotel in down-town Los Angeles, on November 8. He writes, "I made it down here in something like 10 hours less than going up. I got in here at 1630. We didn't lay over any place except Las Vegas…. That was just enough leave to make me homesick, but it certainly was nice to get." He closes with, "Wishing you a happy birthday. Loads of Love, Walter."

"November 12, Dear Folks, today is your Birthday, eh Mom. Received your letter today…. This Battalion has turned in to a sort of Raider affair and we are training as such. Probably we'll go into the fight before the naval barrage even starts & try to knock out the enemy that way – surprise him on a dark night by sneaking in on these boats. Boy will that be rough riding." Walter will not explain his reference to 'these boats' until his next letter, and Myrtle is left in suspense.

Comments like this make me wonder if Walter realizes how much they would worry Myrtle. Here is another example - "A fellow … picked up a 'dud' – the warhead out of a 37 mm shell & … a couple of them were fooling with it in front of the barracks & dropped it. It exploded & nearly blew one of his feet off & tore up the other. Four of the other's feet were seriously injured and two fellows about 100 yds away got shrapnel…. Guess that's about all for now. Love, Walter."

Walter's November 17 letter is hardly reassuring. "Time to write again & again I'm getting back into my Marine mood." Walter's 'Marine mood' is one of complaint and overriding pessimism. To be fair to him, it can certainly be justified.

"Justice died Monday morning at 0515. It really hurt because he was so well known & well liked." A month ago, a couple men were badly injured in an auto accident, and now a corpsman, Justice, has died. "I don't know what he died of, but he did have a fractured scapula, clavicle, fractured skull, possible broken jaw & apparently was bleeding internally. It is very hard to go & collect a fellow's stuff to send home to his widowed mother…. He is the first of the men in the Bn to die since it was formed a year ago."

In several of his previous letters, Walter has expressed doubts that he will survive his enlistment, and during his recent leave he apparently shared those doubts with Myrtle. Now he tries to backpedal. "Really I expect to come back from these maneuvers again. Oh yes you are probably surprised because I said I might be listed among the missing from those rubber boat drills." Myrtle was already aware of his struggles with the Navy's swimming test (he never did pass legitimately) and his description of these drills is not encouraging.

"Either 7 or 10 men, depending on the size of the boat, push it out until the water reaches your chin, then wait till the breaker comes in, then climb in & paddle as hard as possible & be sure to hit the breakers straight. I went out 5 times.... We turned over once but waded back.... I have to go again at night ... with clothes and possibly packs on.... Today we were issued some rubber inflatable pillows about one foot long. Guess they are to be used for buoyancy." Imagining Walter amongst the waves, in the darkness, clutching a foot-long rubber pillow, Myrtle may not be comforted.

"Nov 24, Dear Folks.... I got my allotment started a while back." Walter may be referring to the $3.30/ month premium, automatically deducted from his Navy pay, for his $5,000 life insurance policy. Myrtle is the listed beneficiary. He has attempted to set up a second allotment, directly to Myrtle. That way, when he deploys overseas, she will automatically get a monthly payment.

Now that he has revealed the inherent hazards of the ocean exercises, Walter discusses them in almost a matter-of-fact manner. "You should see us out there trying to ride those rubber boats out to the ocean. Often the waves or breakers come in, probably 10 feet just as they break, and those little rubber boats, some 8 and some 12 feet long, are really tossed around."

"Sometimes fellows are thrown 20 to 30 feet out into space. We had to jump out of our boat after we got past the breakers and turn our boat over to empty it of water. We were fully clothed & had light packs on. I had my small inflatable pillow in my undershirt & it really helped hold me up." Walter seems to be saying – Yes Mother, I know it is dangerous, but I have practiced, I know what to do and it is my duty. Myrtle will still worry, but she understands duty.

For the next two pages, Walter writes about the ranch – the weight of the pigs, Byron's coyote trapping project, and the possible sale of a neighboring ranch. His recent visit may have renewed his connection. He also describes a medical operation, assures them he will send Christmas gifts (a puzzle for David), and promises to send more money home.

His uses his final paragraph to describe his crowded living situation. "The Marines have moved part of the brig into our quarters. Now we have sick bay, sick bay office, O.D. (Officer of the Day?), corpsman's quarters, staff NCO's quarters & now six prisoners, all in a room 32 X 100 ft. Guess that's all right now. Love, Walter."

Twelve days later, December 6th, Walter writes, "Dear Folks… just a note tonight to let you know I'm back after 9 days out. We were aboard a transport, not a bad ship as transports go. The chow was much better than here in camp.

"The Marines made 5 landings, but I only made 3. The first I wasn't sick … on the Higgins boat but the second I got sick… so the Dr. detailed me to stay aboard and run sick bay." Walter notes the time of several of the landings, but his account lacks other details. He does not, for example, describe the Higgins boat, a 36,' barge-like, landing craft, constructed largely of plywood, with an 8,000-pound capacity.

He does provide graphic details, of the Company's final landing, made that very morning, "Started getting aboard the boats at midnight. I got on at 0230 & the whole outfit got lost. We finally landed at 0830 this morning. The water was very rough & about 75% of the fellows got sick. I haven't been so sick & cold before in my life. Vomited till blood came." With boats strung out for 15 miles up and down the beach, the exercise was called off.

"Haven't heard of losing any men. The 23rd Marines lost between 6 & 11 men & over $25,000 worth of equip…. I lost one shoe and one poncho." After their return Walter slept for a few hours, took a hot shower, and then began this letter. He has been sending packages home, some contain presents for the family and others are filled with his personal possessions.

"Dec 10, I'm fine but … but very much behind in my correspondence. I sent off about 20 Christmas cards yesterday – a few more yet." Walter will continue this practice for the next 70 or so years, branching out to include birthday, get well, graduation and sympathy cards.

Walter is working almost exclusively in the office – filing and typing mostly. He has recovered from the exercises and has time for a long letter filled with office gossip about Marines. "They sent in a notice for Munski's transfer – intra regimental. Dr. Porter got hot all over & killed it – Raley left instead. Munski was glad to stay." Minor changes, like the transfer of Raley instead of Munski, can have major consequences. Walter knew both men and much preferred Munski. Munski and Walter will be together through Saipan, Tinian, and Iwo Jima. They will trust and support each other, and after the war will remain friends. Raley, once transferred, will disappear from Walter's life.

Walter has no idea when they may ship out so, just in case, he closes with, "I'm wishing you each a Merry Christmas & will be thinking of you. Love, Walter."

I have to laugh at Walter's next letter. "December 12, Dear Folks, still here so decided to write again. Don't know what has happened since I wrote last." It has only been two days, and the answer seems to be – not much. Walter is still writing and mailing home what personal gear he has left. Raley is still being transferred, and though Walter is glad to have him gone, he resents the fact that "… he got a swell job. Seems like all the gold bricks … are transferred until they hit something soft enough to handle…. Love, Walter."

Around 2100 hours on December 16, Walter manages a four-page letter devoted primarily to the time he has just spent on another transport ship. "This time we were only out 1 day but laid in port for 2 or 3 while the convoy was being made up - surely a large one – ships as far as one could see." When it came time to unload, "The Dr. left me back (with McKay) to bring in the eight sick men & turn them into the Disp." The men were supposed to leave the ship under their own power, but "I knew they were too weak to climb down the nets since they had been in bed 2-3 days and had fevers." The Marine in charge "… couldn't get the Navy officers to lower the men so when it came time I went to the Lt in charge and he loaded my patients in stretchers."

The exercise did not impress Walter. "Boats of all sizes lined up along the beach stranded, the breakers washed them up and they couldn't get off. Tore the ramp off one & broke one of the fellow's arms." Walter was fortunate though. "The water was fairly smooth & I was too busy to get sick."

Walter has been invited to visit the Davis' for a few days over Christmas. "Believe I'll see if I can get a 72 hr. liberty & go down.... Maybe if the PX still has some fancy candied fruit I might take that."

Walter has a new prediction as to when the Division will actually move out. "Bet it won't be till the last of Feb. or first of March – just my latest guess.... Love, Walter."

December 20 - "We drew clothes at 0830 & stood inspection at 1330 also had carbine school at 1330. They want us to have our full quota of clothes now that we are shoving off – just another Marine way – we will pack our sea bags & never see them again – lost.... Right now a flu epidemic is hitting and if many more turn in they will be delayed on sailing."

A few things aren't so bad – "Surely glad I didn't buy a case knife because we've been issued very good ones.... Mrs. Bos sent me a box of swell candy today.... We were paid today." Overall, Walter is doing as well as could be expected as he prepares to ship out for parts unknown.

Naturally, their destination is a source of much speculation and argument among the Corpsmen and Marines. Walter offers his own opinion, which is not close enough to trouble a censor. Censorship will start soon and persist till the summer of 1945.

Walter continues - "My guess is we'll hit Truk – if we do, I'll say something about 'a good guess' near the first of my letter." Truk Atoll, located in the central Pacific northeast of New Guinea, was the site of a major Japanese air and naval base. On February 17, the US Navy launched a massive air and sea attack on the Japanese planes and ships stationed there. This attack was hugely successful, with Japanese losses totaling 250 planes, over 40 ships and 4,500 men. Navy losses were negligible, and the Marines were not involved.

In the meantime, Walter has forms to type and Christmas to spend with Mr. and Mrs. Davis. He says goodbye and assures Myrtle that, "If you don't hear for quite a while, you'll know I have taken a trip. When I do go seems that if you write once a week would be best.... Love, Walter." Walter's penmanship is still good but, perhaps because of the Navy jargon and acronyms, his punctuation and sentence structure have deteriorated. Considering his situation, Miss Fink needs to stop being so picky.

December 24 at the Davis' 'ranch' in La Mesa, Walter writes a short note. "We are sending you 2 boxes of fruit. I picked all except the avocadoes from their orchard." He has picked oranges, lemons, limes, grapefruit, and tangerines. "They tell me the avocadoes are worth 40 cents apiece here now. I wrapped the fruit pretty well and hope it arrives OK."

The next day he writes, "Dearest Folks, it's been Christmas day according to the calendar." He thanks them for their gifts, mostly home baked goods, but also, "...a chess board – Edwards can hardly wait to get started. Several of the boys play but very few boards around .... Will enjoy it pretty soon aboard ship. Each time I write I expect it to be my last. According to all reports we have to be out by the first of the year."

Walter devotes the next two pages to the Davis' opulent lifestyle and their generosity. He has met the rest of the Davis family and many of their friends, and as he says, "They are a swell bunch."

Camp Pendleton is in a turmoil with enlisted men and officers coming and going pretty much as they please. "4 corpsmen didn't come in today – one came in late and went out again, maybe he is leaving the outfit – deserting. Hope one of the fellows does desert.... We got notice today we could take our tests Jan 3 for advancement – wonder if that's Weissman's idea of a joke? ... I have a few more letters to write. Love, Walter."

With 1943 over, Walter has been in the Navy for two years.

I have 214 letters he wrote to the 'Folks' during those two years. He wrote to many others – his two younger brothers, Byron and David, and his uncles and aunts and various other relatives and friends. The pool of correspondents is large, and his wartime letters must number into the thousands.

"Camp Pendleton Jan 4, 1944 Dear Folks, my head is still sort of woozy...." From some Marines, this opening line might hint at a prolonged New Year's Eve binge, but not from Walter. "Can't get off my sea legs. I'm surprised we're back, but then you can never depend on what the Marines will do. I can't understand why we went out. We didn't do anything – bum chow etc."

Walter returns from whatever ship he has been on and finds four letters from Myrtle waiting for him. No doubt they were filled with questions, which he will not address until he laments the loss of his favorite pen. "I broke the clip off & then lost it. I found this cheap pen for 85 cents aboard ship. It will be good enough to go across with." After a half-page about the pen, he rushes through Myrtle's questions.

"Yes, Mother I received 2 fruit cakes – swell too, what little I got of them." He thanks her, again, for the handkerchiefs, the scotch bread, and the chess set, even though, "haven't had any luck on the board – Edwards beat me." I imagine a little impatience in his "Yes, Mother", but Walter remains dutiful.

He describes his holiday with the Davis clan, and then turns to the various quirks and misbehaviors of the other Corpsmen. Guerra went AOL and is on 3-day B&W (bread and water). Cochran, a rebel, has a funny accent. Felicia left on Christmas and never returned. Blevins made chief without taking a test, and later got married "Maybe this week we'll take a test for advancement. I don't plan on making it though."

Rumors continue unabated. "We 'know' (like we know the date of sailing & all other things in the Marine Corps) the place we're going to attack, the number of islands & where each outfit will strike. Maybe our Bn won't even get in the scrap. We'll see." All the men, Walter included, have hidden thoughts, and fears. Each one's future is unknowable, and every scrap of scuttlebutt must be weighed and discussed. The process, though irresistible, can be stressful and frustrating.

"There are so many things I could tell you but forget when I write & other things I just don't say." Walter has edged into dangerous emotional territory and quickly changes the subject.

"I've found a Dago I like – he's a good worker, clean – likes spaghetti dinners with meatballs & a good cigar. He's quite a fellow." Walter has become more accepting of men with different backgrounds and ethnicities, but he still (automatically?) tends to stereotype at first. "It's time for lights out. Love, Walter."

January 10 – "Just a hurried note… Hate to say Wolf, Wolf all the time but we were given a heart to heart talk today. Can't even guess where we're going now but it will be big though, the operation I mean." As the pressure on the men grows, some bend while others break.

"We're right on the spot. A fellow just cut himself badly with his knife." Walter does not elaborate, and his wording makes me wonder if the cut was deliberate. Was this just a different form of 'shooting himself in the foot'?

News from the Davis family brings a trifecta of misery. Someone stole several Christmas presents from their house, among them a $250 watch. Violet's much beloved parrot has died suddenly, and Mr. Davis is scheduled for major surgery.

Walter has his own problem. "Flunked my 1/c test by 0.3 of a point on one subject – clerical forms…. Everything here is swell … Love, Walter." His letter has been almost entirely negative, and I wonder what Myrtle thought about Walter's idea of 'swell.'

PART 6 – SHIPPED OUT – 97 LETTERS
JANUARY 16, 1944 TO AUGUST 31, 1945

"January 18, 1944, Dear Folks, I suppose you would like a note saying I'm well etc. That's about all I have to say." Amazingly, Walter is at sea but not seasick. "Even my headache is nearly gone.... For the first time my tetanus booster didn't make me sick. Will write again when I can. Love Walter." Walter includes his new address, which will remain unchanged for the next year and a half.

Hq Co, 1st Bn 24th Marines

4th Marine Division, FMF

C/o Fleet Post office

San Francisco, Calf.

At this point Walter begins using V-mail. Patterned after the British 'airgraph,' this system greatly reduced the weight of correspondence. Letters are necessarily short since everything, including the address, is written on a 7 x 9 inch form which first goes to the censor and is then photographed. When the thumbnail size negative reaches the US, it will be printed at 2/3 of the original size, placed in a special envelope with a transparent window which reveals the address, and distributed through the USPS without need for a stamp. Walter, while he is aboard ship and during action, uses V-Mail but when the 4th Division returns to Maui after a battle, he often uses the standard red and blue bordered 'via air mail' envelopes which require a six cent stamp.

The convoy arrives in Pearl Harbor January 21, and the next day continues west. Instead of Truk, as Walter predicted a month ago, they head for the Kwajalein Atoll where he will be part of the assault on the twin islands of Roi-Namur.

When Walter writes again on February 5, the battle is over. Here is his V-mail letter in its entirety. "Dear Folks, just a note to tell you all is quiet here now. Guess you know about as much about this as we do. Would like to see the movie - more fun than being here. Nothing but one sniper that shot at me. I got a little sunburned. All of our corpsmen and doctors came out OK – guess one corpsman is up for a citation. Twenty of us went up where he was the first night as stretcher bearers. A scary job but no one shot at me. It's a terrible job going around picking up the decomposed Jap bodies. I'll write a little in a few days. Been a month since we've received any mail. Send me a couple newspapers dated Feb 1-5. Love, Walter."

Walter has used 'terrible' many times in his letters. He has used it to describe San Diego street- walkers, substandard Navy butter, and a movie he didn't like. He has used it for a broken window and for the death of a sailor whose appendix ruptured. If I visualize the sight and smell of thousands of bloated, putrefying bodies and their assorted parts, rotting in the hot tropical sun, imagine him having to handle, pick up, and dispose of same, then 'terrible,' in its full meaning, seems appropriate.

D- Day on Roi-Namur was January 31, although Naval shelling and air strikes had been going on for days. Beach landings on Roi itself began February 1. Opposition on Roi was relatively light, and early February 2 it was declared secure. Namur presented more of a challenge, but organized Japanese resistance was soon over. American casualties amounted to 190 killed and 547 wounded. Out of almost 3,500 Japanese on the twin islands less than 100 survived, a casualty rate greater than 97%. A casualty rate in the nineties is exceptionally high, but in the coming battles of Saipan, Tinian and Iwo Jima, the Japanese will suffer similar loses.

One major reason for these high casualties is indoctrination. The average Japanese soldier at this time was the product of a military philosophy that glorified a twisted form of the samurai tradition. Beginning near the end of the nineteenth century, Japanese military theory held that the 'yamato damashi,' or 'fighting spirit,' of the Japanese warrior would always triumph. Encouraged by their 1905 success in the Russo-Japanese war and their subsequent seizure of Korea, the military dominated the government, even though their constitution gave authority to their god-emperor. However, Emperor Hirohito had been relentlessly indoctrinated almost since birth to believe that it was Japan's destiny to become a great imperial power because of their inherent yamato damashi.

For the average Japanese soldier, military service was brutal. Recruits often received daily beatings for any or no reason. Men were forced to practice beheading and bayonetting on Chinese civilians and captured enemy soldiers. Absolute obedience to orders was both a soldier's duty and his honor. Surrender for any reason was specifically forbidden. If a Japanese soldier had the misfortune to be captured while unconscious, it was his duty to kill himself when he awoke. Fighting to the death in a hopeless situation was considered a necessity, especially for Japanese officers. Walter had of course heard stories about suicidal Japanese soldiers, but on Roi-Namur he witnessed it.

On February 6, the day after he mentioned his 'terrible job,' Walter writes a light, reassuring letter. It is almost as though nothing has happened. "Boy I feel fine now – 3 good meals and a couple good night's sleep in our foxhole. We have a super deluxe one now.... We're on Namur a very small spot here in the Marshalls.... I carried a .45 this time – lost my carbine the first day & didn't look for it. The pistol was much handier.... Boy it's fun swimming here in the ocean or lagoon swell climate. Bet you'd like a little of it right now. Love, Walter." Now that he is in salt water, Walter, who could not legitimately pass the Navy's swimming test, is getting around fine. He does not mention the Japanese corpses again, but the memories will torment him for decades.

By February 8, the convoy is on the move, and Walter does not write till they dock, Feb 23. "Dear Folks, I can't say where I'm at but at least we don't have to be afraid to move about the camp after dark. Want to wish Dad a happy birthday a little early. Over here grapefruit is so sweet sugar is not necessary. Haven't eaten the other fruit yet. Very little liberty. Love, Walter."

They are on Maui, 1,800 feet above sea level, but Walter cannot reveal his location to his folks. For the next three months Camp Maui will pass for 'home' for the Fourth Marines. When Walter arrives construction is in the early stages. Even finished, the camp will consist of little more than Quonset huts and 16-foot square wall-tents.

Walter's February 25 letter edges toward normal. He begins with some family news, includes a bit of scuttlebutt, and offers encouragement to his brother Byron. Walter seems more relaxed, perhaps because he has been paid, and so has plenty of money for now.

He has been forced to give up the .45 pistol though, which apparently wasn't his to begin with. "Surely wish I could get another; they are so much handier than the carbine.... picked up a Jap ash tray I'd like to send home but will have to find out the regulations first.

"Certainly wish I hadn't sent all of the material in my note book home. Now I have to get busy and work it all out again. I must work on forms too. Just pray that nothing happens to Dr. Porter – he will take care of us. Boy it hurt him to send us out to the front.... Love, Walter."

Walter has worked well with many doctors, and two of them, Dr. Shiring and Dr. Porter, are with the Fourth Marines now. A good doctor, I imagine, would become very protective of his corpsmen, and the corpsmen would be extremely loyal. This appears to be the dynamic between Walter and Dr. Porter.

The last of February, leap-day, Walter writes, "Just back from liberty. It was a very quiet one. The Bn. furnished transportation to a Country Club and from there we hitchhiked around a bit.... It's really pretty out here.... Got another bottle of vitamin pills. Things like that are very expensive here. Guess I'll sign off. Love Walter."

Walter will write from the camp on Maui through March, April and the first ten days of May. Camp construction will continue even longer, more Quonset huts will be erected, and electrical service extended. It will remain a work in progress for four and a half months and Walter will contribute his share. "I started a table for the office, took me 5 days to finish it ... nothing for looks but seems quite stable."

On other subjects, "Guess if I ever see anything like a book store I'll get a dictionary. We have some terrible times with some words & you know what my spelling has always been like. Byron couldn't have seen me in that picture because I definitely was not in it.... Wednesday, I saw some snaps of the island and the action. Boy, but I'd like to have some of the more horrible ones, really what war is like."

Working with Munski, Walter has been able to scrounge some choice items. "Already we have a hammer, candles & other items not to be publicized. Love, Walter."

Walter's Maui letters are a mixture. Some are on V-Mail, while others he writes on standard size 'onion skin' paper and sends by stamped airmail.

"March 10, I intended to wait & write you after we were paid & include a couple money orders." The corpsmen are paid in cash and to avoid the nuisance of buying and mailing money orders home, Walter requested an 'allotment' months ago. It has not gone through so he must fuss with money orders.

"Raley really surprised the boys, gave me $2 to pay off one of his debts to a fellow." This is a surprise and is the first and last good thing Walter ever writes about Raley.

"Had some swell eats the other day on liberty, banana splits & a glass of milk until I almost split too. Love Walter."

"March 12, Dear Folks, as long as I'm sending the money orders might as well include a note. Tonight we have electric lights, nice huh?" It has taken about two months for Camp Maui to get power. Eleven years will pass before the ranch gets AC service.

"Funny little note in the paper tonight. Someone approved the plan to send WAACs to Hawaii – but they couldn't go swimming because no one has created official bathing suits for them yet."

Pop's birthday is approaching, and Water writes, "... wonder if you'll have the usual bad weather the 13?" Of course, predicting bad weather in Montana during March is not much of a stretch.

"March 16, 1944, Dear Folks, … I should be telling you what I did on liberty, but the colonel restricted the Bn. so we have to stand more inspections."

Walter and some other corpsmen have been at the store stocking up on fruit, fresh and canned. "Now an order came out we aren't allowed to have any in our tents. I'll have to stage a party and get rid of the stuff."

Walter reports on his health. "I have been having trouble with my bowels, first time in my life." Otherwise, he is fine and even has access to a radio. "Very nice to hear one again also commentators on the war. Guess the war is still going on out there too isn't it?

"Guess I'll try for 1/c again March 23. Certainly hope I can make it. There is certainly an awful pile to learn… Love, Walter."

Walter's March 23 V-Mail is typed, and the filming/reprinting/reduction process hasn't helped. On the folds, parts are completely illegible. Phrases jump out: "test postponed … tomorrow … 40 questions…. If we ever get back to civilization. Regiment … seems … games … sick bay … moved … 4 times … nice chow…plates… all kinds of weather…. Love, Walter."

His March 24 V-Mail is hand written. "No Mom, there's nothing you can send me. Believe we can get more things here than you can, maybe you'd better send your shopping list to me… my exam was scheduled for tonight, again it was postponed. Likely will be given too late to be rated next month even if I do pass the test. Such is life out here. Love Walter."

In his March 28 letter Walter describes the destruction that took place on Roi-Namur and explains that the dead were buried, not thrown into the ocean. He has passed the 1/c test and immediately minimizes his achievement. "Took all day but really wasn't so hard, there would have been no excuse if I hadn't passed it…. Don't know when the rate will go into effect. Gee I get tired of these poker games especially when they are in our tent… It makes such a mess to clean up next morning."

On March 30, back from one of his rare liberties, he writes again. He found the towns very crowded. "I'll bet these people here will be almost as glad to see us leave as we will to go." He has been unable to find anyone who can remove and clean the face of his wrist watch.

"Did a funny thing, bought a scarf for a table… but won't be able to send it home because of the geographic pictures on it. I wrote Aunt Sjaan one day & received a letter from her 2 days later. Glad to hear you got the money OK. Love, Walter." I get the feeling Walter prefers using the V-Mail sheets. Besides being free, they are short, and if he does not feel like writing, it is easy for him to fill a page.

His April 2 letter runs for three pages. Walter begins with the weather. "Sometimes I think that the place might be nice, but I don't like the suddenness or violence of the storms." This is hardly surprising, since he is living in a tent.

Although Walter has passed the test for 1/c, his rating has not gone through because "…the report of advancement wasn't typed out perfect but previously they went thru OK…. Seems that from the division on down they can't agree on how many & which forms to send. We thought we had all of our reports prepared & then another interpretation came & we had to prepare another kind. I'll bet the divisional office is a mess."

"Don't believe I told you Comdr. Eddie Peabody & group were here the other night & put on a performance. It was good. The extent can be judged by the reaction of our colonel – he laughed. I hear that he did that once before." Peabody was a very popular banjo player and showman who re-joined the Navy to entertain the troops.

Walter, on page three now and still going strong, takes up the subject of money. "This is one place where the fellows don't complain about not having enough money. Very few things to spend it on…. Funny in spite of this I had over $46 loaned out. All but 5 came back yesterday on a small payday…. We'll probably be paid again about April 5, so I'll probably send more home then. Certainly wish the allotment had gone through."

Finally, Walter notes that they have had a real inspection – by a general, no less. After three pages he ends with, "Bet this length has been a surprise to you, to me also – Goodnight, Walter."

Walter's V-Mail of April 9, Easter Sunday, is subdued. They have been on Maui about 1½ months and a sort of languor has set in. "Rather quiet in camp as it is regular liberty day for most." He has found a watch repair shop and writes, "Hope they don't spoil it. So far … it keeps perfect time. Today I packed up some of the Jap objects to send home & probably will…. Will have to get busy and type out my form for advancement one of these days too." Hardly the words of a man anxious for a pay raise.

Somehow, Myrtle has assumed Walter has been in another assault and in his April 11, letter, he sets her straight. "You must want us to get this war over in a hurry to think we were in those last invasions. Give us time, we'll shove off for xxxxxx." Walter has blacked out the word, as he says, to "Save him *(the censor)* the trouble." Walter does not know where he is bound, but in any case, such speculations do not belong in a letter.

"No, don't send me anything to eat. We get fine chow at this NCO mess, if you could see me, you'd know how fat I am. Sometimes it takes a month for a package to get here & if we move farther away, even longer." As to what the future holds, "The boys have a rhyme 'see the Golden Gate in 48; the bread line in 49.' I wonder? I sent the souvenirs on their way April 9. Love, Walter."

April 18 Walter writes, "Well we're back again…. I enjoyed the first 5 miles. Of course I can't say what we saw except that the machinery was interesting, yes & we saw a couple white women!" Despite the censors, an astute reader of Walter's letters could reasonably infer that he is in the Pacific on a tropical island with a largely non-white population and an advanced agricultural economy.

He has been on Maui for about two months, and writes, "This was my first hike since we arrived, but I stood up just as well as many who have made all of them. Of course, several fell out for various reasons This morning we got up about 0330 & ate, then laid around until 0900 & started for camp.

"Our corpsman, Jack Gottlieb, is a botanist. Learned a few little things from him. Saw the flower mentioned in 'Dragonwyck.' Have been reading a few books lately." Whether Walter actually has developed a taste for gothic romance novels, or only took up Anya Seton's 419 page work out of boredom, I cannot say. However, the flower mentioned in Dragonwyck is oleander, common to Maui. Moving on to non-poisonous plants, he asks, "Are you going to plant all of the lower potato patch this year?... Will probably send a money order tomorrow if we get paid. Love, Walter."

On April 20, over three weeks early to allow for any delays, Walter sends a Mother's Day card. The card, with its pink roses on the front and saccharine verse inside, would be ordinary but for the presence, all in shiny silver, of an embossed eagle, wings outspread, perched atop a shield adorned with thirteen stars. Regardless, his words to Myrtle inside the card ring true. "All my love, Walter."

In his V-Mail of April 23rd Walter downplays the two-day problem they have just completed. "Wasn't especially tired after the hike.... Fired the rife from the hip... now comes the job of cleaning the thing. This trip was all more fun than most... told before we went that the place was going to be very rugged and miserable because it was so wet, wasn't as bad as I anticipated .... Some of the fellows didn't fix up their tents right so the water did run in during the night but that was their own fault.... Being paid tomorrow, I guess. I should draw $145 this time."

In the midst of the war Walter still thinks about maintenance on the ranch. "Has Byron ridden around the fences this year or are you going to try to keep them up? Was wondering how the fence over by the school section was holding up. Love, Walter"

"Camp, April 29, Dear Folks, I have 3 regular & 2 V mail letters on hand." It has been less than a week since his last letter, so mail delivery is surely sporadic. "Well we had another liberty... got my watch back but they were unable to open it, so guess I'll have to carry on. It still works OK."

Walter answers a question about his pay. "2/c draw $96 base pay, overseas increases it 20% so that makes me $115.20 per month. My insurance costs $3.20 I believe. By the way I took out $5,000 more in Pop's name. If my next rate goes thru then my base pay would be about $113. Am sending along $100 money order.

"Received some new corpsmen today, right at the end of the month so now I have to change all of the reports. They are getting a good initiation – they're told we're going out right away, - or that we all have to make a 63-mile hike in 36 hours etc. They do seem to be scared of the idea of going into combat. Too soft a life so far, I'm afraid."

"Camp May 4, 1944. Dear Folks, Yesterday was liberty day so there was lots of work piled up in the office today… we are very busy." Walter has been on Maui for over two months and his days have fallen into a routine. Paperwork – the endless, ever changing, forms and reports that are the Navy's lifeblood – occupies his duty hours.

Because he does not drink, smoke, or gamble Walter continues to send money home - $90 this time – close to a month's pay. To occupy his free time, he reads, watches an occasional movie, and writes letters. "I had fun on liberty yesterday. We started out at 0845 & and it was 1030 by the time we got off our second bus. A swell drive & a nice town. Almost no servicemen, so the people and town were nice." Walter closes in a reflective mood. "To stay here so long gets tiresome but to go aboard ship to get away is worse for me, sort of a bad place to be. Last time I missed out on a lot happening on the beach because I was sick in the landing boat – guess it's all part of war though. Goodbye, Walter."

Walter is caught in a pattern common to many military situations, in which soldiers are subject to alternating periods of boredom and extreme stress. This time a year ago, Walter was at Camp Pendleton where he was often bored. When it finally came, the fight for Roi-Namur, lasted only a few days. Since then he has been waiting on Maui for almost three months. It is a serene, beautiful place, a literal 'tropical paradise.' He cannot fully relax because he knows that more battles await him. He must know that the Fourth Marine Division was not created solely for the one week assault on Roi-Namur.

The upcoming assault on Saipan and Tinian, will be a longer, bloodier operation. Afterward the Marines will return to Camp Maui, this time for five months of rest, and yes, boredom. The battle of Iwo Jima, when it comes in February of 1945, will be worse than anything they have experienced. By the time Iwo Jima is history Walter will have repeatedly experienced long periods of boredom interrupted by moments of sheer terror. He will not emerge undamaged.

On the surface, Walter's V-Mail of Monday, May 8, is unremarkable. He has probably spent another day pushing paper and just needs to clean his rifle, something he has been putting off, and go to bed. He is bothered though because "...the Regiment pulled a raw deal on some of our boys, none of the fellows up for 1/c passed. Gottlieb was one who rates it as much as any man ... but they flunked him & passed one of their boys that doesn't even know as much as I do." Although a senior corpsman, he is still modest about his own abilities. He knows 'our boys' and after their shared time on Roi-Namur, he is outraged by favoritism and injustice.

May 11th Walter sends another V-Mail in which, for the only time I can remember, he brags about breaking military regulations. "We had some fun yesterday dodging the MPs and SPs. We wanted to get into a store for some fruit but were not in the uniform of the day. I got some but had to use some back alleys though.... Goodbye, Walter." To men about to assault a fortified island, the Marine dress code might seem unimportant or even silly.

I have a niggling question. At this point Walter has written about 240 letters to the folks on the ranch. He nearly always closes 'Love, Walter' though there are a handful of 'Love to all' and 'All my love.' However, his two previous letters, and this one, all end with a stark "Goodbye, Walter." Is he aware of the change or is this a difference that doesn't matter?

His next letter, also a V-Mail, is dated simply 'May.' "Guess it's about time I wrote again, sort of hard to find something to say. We've gotten down to the place where we're trying to decide when a person can no longer be called a 'foreigner'." Walter raises a serious question, one of extreme interest to many immigrants, and especially to Americans of Japanese and German heritage who may worry about their future in America. I wonder what Walter thought.

"Haven't received a letter for some time so have no hint to write on from one of yours.... It would be nice to go to Australia for our next rest camp after we make our next landing. Probably won't be consulted on the matter so will enjoy the sights as much as possible as we go along. Love, Walter"

On May 25 he fills two pages. By this date, they have moved from Maui to Pearl Harbor. He begins with a puzzler: "Just got liberty over with, a terrible ordeal but seems we all try it." Then he second guesses himself. "I often wonder just what would have happened if I'd joined the Army as I'd started to. Certainly no worse off & the more I see, the more it looks like a soft racket."

Walter manages to put aside whatever is troubling him and focuses on the ranch. Now he seems specific and engaged, even mentioning one horse by name. "Have you got 3 mowers now? Need some hired help to keep all the equipment on the go, three mowers and a rake.... Sort of miss Nellie, ornery as she was."

A discussion with David confirmed that all the ranch machinery was still horse drawn, and in 1952 I watched Walter harness King, the last of the workhorses, to pull the potato digger up and down the rows in Myrtle's huge garden.

While Walter has been writing, the others have been painting the town. "Hearns & his gang are back so will quit. Certainly they had a time & surprisingly enough the M.P.s didn't pick them up. Love, Walter."

May 27, two days before they ship out, Walter manages to dash off a V-Mail. "Dear Folks, Seems the Marine Corps is outdoing itself being nice to us all of a sudden. Have been making the most of it too. Out again today with Munski & Zaar and visited the base hospital. Today we saw Erikson (came from Bremerton with him) & he told me he had seen DeVore at Pearl Harbor & heard that Rickard was in charge of some sort of a supply depot there. He believes Lloyd may be there now, leave it to him to get good duty.

"Everybody around here is about half drunk tonight. Just back from a beer party the Bn. had today, plenty of beer, I guess. Love, Walter."

Over the month of June, Walter only writes twice, both V-Mails, on June 5th and 6th. "June 5, 1944, Dear Folks, have been planning to write ever since Memorial Day but it is so easy to put off because there is nothing more to say one day than the last. We can say now that we are aboard ship on our way to our destination. Of course, this won't be mailed for several days.... Somehow, I don't feel as excited as last time, in fact no one does of the older group. At times, a group of 25 – 50 men will sit or stand around without saying anything for half an hour at a time. The exception is a group of new corpsmen we got in just before we left & they're so full of play and noise it bothers at times." The older corpsmen have already seen combat and have an idea of what they will face on Saipan. No wonder the levity of the newbies is annoying.

In reality, the assault on Saipan will be much worse, more intense, and bloodier than the three days spent on Roi-Namur. Under the command of General H.M. Smith, the Marines are attempting to follow a battle plan that has them taking the island in just three days. U.S. military intelligence is badly mistaken, and the assault will last three and a half weeks.

Walter quickly changes the subject to the ranch and writes, "By the time this gets there you will have started haying. Has that dodder spread any more through the alfalfa?" Haying on the ranch usually begins sometime in the last week of June. Dodder, a weed of the morning glory family, outlasted the war and was still a nuisance in the 1950s when I lived on the ranch.

Walter concludes, "This paper is so damp it makes the writing rather fuzzy. Would surely be nice to find a cool dry spot. Love, Walter."

"June 6th, Dear Folks, believe this will be my last note before we make our landing. Sort of tired of reading…. I know you are very busy, but I wish you would get "Winter Wheat' & read it. It wasn't written quite as well as 'A Tree Grows in Brooklyn' but I liked the story better.

"Today a destroyer came along side and transferred a sick sailor to this ship for an appendectomy. Of course, they didn't stop just pulled up beside us & continued…. Well the speaker system says 'Prepare to darken ship' so guess I'll go up above & cool off a bit. May be some time before I write again. Love, Walter." Walter will not write again until July 9, and by then the Battle for Saipan, which began June 15, will be officially over.

Walter's V-Mail of July 9 begins as usual. "Dear Folks, probably by this time you know we are on Saipan. It's been very hard going but up to now I've stayed with the outfit, no injuries, not even had my clothes torn off.... Funny I dreamed that David was hurt on his birthday. He so often does get hurt on his birthday or special day. I was wondering if it happened this time.... Gosh, it would be nice to be back there where it's not so hot & damp and just a little quiet for a time. Love, Walter."

Overall, 3,000 Marines died and 13,000 were wounded on Saipan. On the morning of July 7, when it was clear they were defeated, a ragged group of about 4,000 desperate Japanese launched what proved to be the largest banzai charge of the entire war. The charge penetrated the left flank of the 27th Army Division and was finally stopped by Marines fairly close to Walter's position.

By July 9, less than 1,000 of the original 30,000 Japanese soldiers on Saipan are still alive. The others have died in battle or committed suicide. By their pointless sacrifice they have shown their loyalty to the god-emperor and achieved 'gyokusai.' Literally meaning 'jade shards,' it refers to the destruction of something of great value just to keep someone else from having it. For the survivors it has been a deafening, stinking, hellish 24 days, and they will carry it with them for the rest of their lives.

On July 13, with the battle essentially over, Walter writes another V-Mail. "Dear Folks, Last night part of us moved back to a bivouac area and dug in. We thought for the first time we'd get a full night's sleep... Plane woke us up about 0100 & we couldn't sleep for a while. It is quiet though."

Much of this short letter is a sort of crop report. Sugar cane, pineapples, corn, wild cotton, peanuts, bananas, tobacco, and sweet potatoes all grow in the rocky soil. Leave it to a farmer to notice such things. Walter closes with "Took a shower this morning – first time in 10 days. Came ashore with new shoes but now the heels are worn out. You know there doesn't seem much to say. I received Byron's letter. Love, Walter."

"Saipan Island July 16, 1944, Dear Folks, I feel pretty good now after a couple full night's sleep in a fly proof, rain proof, foxhole. Why we made a foxhole I'm not sure unless it's because we don't feel safe topside. It's about 2' deep lined with corrugated roofing iron with a rounded roof high enough to sit up in.... Here was the first time we even took off our shoes during the whole operation. Japs came into our company area quite often at night."

Walter has been thinking about death as a sort of mysterious harvester of the lives of young men. "Yesterday, a month to the hour, I went back to the beach where we landed & covered the ground that was so hard to get over then.... went to attend the funeral ceremony, an awful lot of our boys down there. Strange how they were picked, and we were left."

Two days later, sounding somewhere between somber and bitter, he finishes the letter. "Some of the boys looking thru their seabags have found everything spoiled... dropped in the ocean in handling. I was lucky, everything of mine is here and OK. Maybe next time I'll be evacuated & lose it all. That doesn't seem important & over here if one lost his best pen or watch he hardly notices it. I just hope I'm not hit in the abdomen. At least if evacuated you're thru with the Marine Corps for a while." There is some truth in Walter's morbid observation.

"Gosh but I enjoy that Time magazine, all of the corpsmen do. This last one got away from me before I finished it. Hope you're finished with most of the haying by the time this get there. Love, Walter."

On July 21, six days after the battle has been declared over, but still on Saipan, Walter describes a disturbing incident. "The other night 3 Japs came up into the company area to get a drink of water. The guard asked them what they were doing and of course they didn't answer. He said something else & still no answer so in true Marine fashion asked for the password. Then the Japs started to run, he fired but didn't get them."

These three men could have been soldiers, but it is more likely they were civilians. Between 25,000 and 40,000 peasants - men, women, and children, were living and working on the island when the Marines landed. Some were Japanese, but there were also Okinawan, Taiwanese, Korean, and even a couple thousand indigenous Chamorros. About 15,000 were taken into custody by US forces and survived. The rest, whether 10,000 or some larger number, died on Saipan. There is photographic evidence that as many as 5,000 may have committed suicide by leaping from cliffs that overlooked the sea. The others, thousands of them, men, women, and children, apparently died in the fighting, killed by one side or the other. Some were probably burned to death by Marines while hiding in shelters that looked like bunkers.

Walter continues, "On this last operation the next of kin of the evacuated & wounded were notified if a man had only a slight wound." Walter will remember this Marine policy, and later, when he catches a small piece of shrapnel in one arm, he will remove it himself to avoid being put in for a Purple Heart. He does not want to worry Myrtle. He puts the letter aside overnight and finishes it on July 22, with what may be a joke. "It's raining right now so the only people out are those taking a shower. Think I'll write a V-Mail and then quit for a while. Love, Walter."

On July 23, Walter and the rest of the men will board their various ships. The next day they will begin their assault on the island of Tinian, conveniently located just three miles from Saipan. Walter will not write again till August 4.

When he was in his nineties, Walter began to tell a few stories about his experiences during the war. He described the carnage on the Saipan beach as terrible. The noise from artillery rounds, flying in both directions, was deafening and Walter suffered some permanent hearing loss. He remembers kneeling on the beach tending to a Marine whose leg looked like 'raw hamburger.' He had just cleaned the wound as much as possible when "… a shell, I think it was from an old WW1 artillery piece, landed. The blast knocked me out and the next thing I remember, I was on my feet swearing a blue streak. The man's leg I had just cleaned was completely covered with sand. There was nothing I could do." He told this story several times, almost exactly word for word.

A year or so before he died, Dad told me another Saipan story. "The Marines had set up a C.P. in a farmhouse on the edge of a sugarcane field. On the other side it was all jungle with snipers. We had a lot of casualties. There was a rumor the Japs were bringing up a tank and if they did, I figured we were all dead. There was a colonel in the farmhouse, and he was almost hysterical. He was slurring his words and I think he was drunk. He started yelling 'Charge!' It would have been suicide to charge. Nobody charged. The Jap tank never showed up." I waited, expectant, but Dad had dozed off. I never heard that story again.

On paper, the assault on Tinian pales when compared to the battle for Saipan. Officially declared over on August 1, the battle results in 394 American Marines KIA and 1,961 wounded. The proximity of the two islands greatly assists the assault. During the battle for Saipan, Naval batteries have been bombarding Tinian's defenses. Meanwhile, US planes gather valuable intelligence and bomb airfields and other targets. Japanese defenders on Tinian numbered about 9,000, less than a third of those on Saipan. The battle ends with only 252 prisoners, the rest are dead, except for a very few who flee into the mountains. Civilian deaths are estimated at 4,000 out of an original 10,000 to 15,000 residents.

Nevertheless, the Japanese fight fiercely, and it is for his actions here that Walter is awarded his first Bronze Star. The citation reads in part, "For heroic achievement in action against the enemy on Tinian on 25 July 1944. PhM1/c Dodd, when all the corpsmen in one of the rifle companies were either killed or wounded, observed a jeep ambulance, the driver of which was fatally wounded. With complete disregard for his own safety, he jumped into the jeep and drove it through intense enemy fire to the aid of the most exposed casualties. Ignoring the heavy fire, he placed the wounded in the ambulance and removed them to a place of safety."

Walter's 'Enlisted Man's Jacket' contains Navy form 'NAVPERS-601(9-43) showing two recommendations, likely for this same incident. One, dated 8 September, is for the Bronze Star Medal for 'meritorious achievement while serving with a Marine division.' The second recommendation, dated 12 September, is for the Silver Star for 'heroic achievement evacuating wounded from the front lines under heavy enemy fire.' So, which medal does he deserve, Bronze or Silver?

For perspective, consider the casualty figures on Tinian. In figuring casualties, the Marines give dead and wounded an equal weight, so to them, casualties among the corpsmen were almost identical to those of the entire Battalion. If we look only at deaths, the story changes dramatically. Thirty one of the Battalion's 613 men, or 5%, died on

Tinian. Of the Battalion's twenty six corpsmen, five, or close to 20% were killed in action. Despite this evidence of the corpsmen's extra risk, Walter receives a Bronze.

August 4, three days after Tinian was declared secured, Walter completes a V-Mail. "Tinian Island, Dear Folks, for some unknown reason I came through this campaign without a scratch, didn't even get sick this time. I'm back at the bivouac area supposedly taking it easy but you should see the sick call. Seems that every little scratch gets infected. I lost my rifle on D plus 1, but other than that still have all my equipment. Sort of wanted to go back and get it but the one I picked up was much better."

Walter does not mention 'evacuating the wounded' or 'heavy enemy fire' – Myrtle worries enough as it is – and quickly changes the subject. "Guess by now it's getting sort of hot at home. Oh yes be sure & save me plenty of those strawberry preserves. Maybe you could send me some when we get somewhere else. Packages are not delivered here. Love, Walter."

On August 7, just before leaving Tinian, Walter pens a V-Mail. He says little and uses half a page to explain the proper way to abbreviate his mailing address. He also says he saw a movie.

August 25, eighteen days later he writes again. "Dear Folks, haven't written for a long time but this should explain much of it. We are now back at our rest camp – boy does this fresh clean air smell & feel good. Showers of fresh water – seems like living again. Many times, I wasn't sure I'd ever see it again." He has been in transit aboard ship. Now he is back on Maui, and living in a tent with rudimentary amenities, yet he is grateful. This is understandable if we consider that for the past three months, he has been either aboard ship or in combat.

Walter does not provide graphic details of the fighting, probably so as not to alarm his folks more than necessary. Counting civilians, as many as 65,000 people died on those islands in two months. Walter has seen much of this and acted with bravery and a certain disregard for his own safety. From his letters, it is obvious that he does not feel he can tell his parents.

His August 25 letter continues, "Of course first day back & the Reg. has us down & gives us a pep talk & assignment of work. Lots of purple hearts & back reports to catch up on." Just like that, Walter goes from dodging sniper fire and nursing wounded Marines, to pushing paper.

He thanks Myrtle for her letters and remarks that, "I find that my clothes are all large for me, even my tailored Marine Greens." He also notices, "The boys here in the rear echelon look so pale & also very clean. Perhaps we will be like that soon. You know already the operation is beginning to seem distant." After covering some family happenings, he offers one more bit of reassurance – ostensibly to Myrtle, but perhaps also to himself. "There's nothing wrong with me now, I believe, that some good food and rest won't cure. Wish I could get some of your cooking now." He closes in his usual fashion with "Love, Walter."

Walter's September 2 letter is about everything and everyone except himself. He is trying to fix reports that were either messed up or not submitted at all during his absence. He has been writing daily, including what he calls "… another 'hard to write' letter to a corpsman's mother and sister. Wish I could tell you a bit about the corpsmen, sort of keep you up to date." When a corpsman is killed, someone needs to write a personal letter to the family.

Myrtle must have lots of questions, and Walter gives them an entire page. He makes a few references to Neil, Munski and a couple of other corpsmen, before asserting, "Believe this covers a little of everything, Love, Walter."

Walter's V-Mails are becoming rare now that he is on Maui, but on September 7 he writes another. He is caught up on most of his correspondence and is even getting close to straightening out the reports that were messed up or not filed while he was gone.

He writes, "Yesterday I went on my first liberty & pretty well supplied myself. Noticed a change in personnel in some of the (civilian) stores. Never figured I would be able to tell one person from another or remember these faces." Walter is making progress – not all the Hawaiians look alike to him now.

When he writes from 'rest camp' on September 14, his life has returned to normal. The mail is still slow and erratic, the paperwork remains frustrating, and the camp lights still fail many nights.

However, "…tomorrow I must write a very hard letter in answer to one from a casualty's folks." This is the second time Walter mentions these 'hard letters' and each one must be like a punch in the gut, knocking him back into the battles, the noise, the blood and the dead, forcing him to remember what he would rather forget.

"September 19, Dear Folks, just a note to enclose the 4 money orders. A swell pay check. Still have plenty…. Mother, I'm going to send you some pictures to try to prove that I'm OK." Walter is apparently under maternal inquisition, and knowing Myrtle, it is relentless. Still, Walter brought this on himself when, a couple letters ago, he let slip the fact that his clothes are too large.

In case the photo does not do the trick, he tries a diversion: "I believe a well packed fruit cake would come through OK. Love, Walter." This is a win-win solution. Myrtle will have something to do, and as for Walter? He will probably manage a slice or two before 'the boys' descend like locusts.

On September 24, Walter writes again. Things are quiet and he has had to "…rewrite a form for the doctor. He signed his name with his middle initial instead of his full name."

In good news, "Munski moved into the tent. I believe we will be well supplied with fruit juice & extras that his brother can pick up at the Army." The prospect of two Munskis operating in inter-service cooperation could shock even a Navy chief into sobriety.

Walter reflects, "Just 2 months ago today we were on the beach at Tinian. Some things seem like yesterday & others are past history now." Parts of the past, especially happenings during the island assaults, will torment Walter for years. Right now though he has letters to answer. "Guess I'll write a couple V. Mails … Love, Walter."

"Camp, September 28, Dear Folks, … Gee it would be nice to be there & feel the frost." A September frost is normal in Montana, and it has been nearly a year since he last saw the ranch. He shipped out from San Diego almost nine months ago and as the war drags on, he wonders, "…if this thing will ever be over – guess that's about the only way to get home."

Walter is frustrated. When he enlisted on January 1, 1942, it was for a period of two years. In just over three months, he will begin his fourth year. Iwo Jima is still ahead of him, and if he survives that landing, he could remain with the Fourth Marines. With Japanese soldiers fighting to the last man, the Marines expect to assault the Home Islands. There the Japanese resistance will be the strongest and most fanatical. The promised two-year duty has proved to be, like some other wartime promises, worthless.

Compared to his possible future, Maui isn't bad at all and Walter tries to sound positive, "The boys have a phonograph with a couple of albums, and we have hot water showers for headquarters company. We may deposit money with the Govt at 4% compound interest – the only thing is it can't be drawn out until discharged. Say I didn't tell you- I went out & knocked a golf ball around 9 holes the other day. With a little practice I might be able to get by." Walter has put up a good front, but as he closes his feelings are laid bare. "Some of the parents haven't heard yet that their sons were killed on Tinian. It's terrible. Love, Walter."

Tucked in among Walter's September 1944 letters is a solitary penny post card dated September 27 and addressed to Myrtle Dodd. The card is from Myrtle's cousin Violet Davis and is presumably typical of Violet's style of correspondence. Violet writes, "My dearest Myrtle – Dear please forgive me - I haven't been able to write to anyone. Not even our dear boy Walter. He's such a dear boy, and I read such a dear letter from him. Bless his heart. All my love to you all, Violet." That Walter was willing to correspond with Violet for over three years, seems to me a tribute to his good manners and kindness.

"Camp, October 4, Dear Folks, I have four of your unanswered letters here & some others so guess I'd better get busy. So finally our canyon has become contaminated with blackleg." Myrtle has apparently delivered the bad news. Blackleg is a bacterial disease of cattle and sheep that is highly fatal. Its spores can remain in the soil over time and once an area is contaminated, vaccination becomes a necessity.

Walter sees death and suffering everywhere, even in an official Marine publication. "Today saw one of those yearbooks that I bought. Not so many of those faces with us now – transferred or evacuated or left behind. A man came back from the army hospital today with the recommendation he use a hearing aid. Some dope for a man in combat."

Walter could ride a horse around the island, "but the price is terrific - $3 the first hr. & $2.50 thereafter. Soon buy a horse at that rate. Some of the boys went on a beer party the other day & rounded up a stray horse & really laid themselves out. Fell off in all sorts of piles.

"Received a letter from Murrell today. Of all things that really seem idiotic to us, he is complaining. We say we would take any kind of duty stateside without griping but guess his case sort of proves a point or two. Looks like an entire new regime will take over the 1st Bn. We have a C.O. in Hq Co now from a sort of Post troop unit so can expect some rigid inspections & lots of 'ideas.' About enough for now. Love, Walter."

Walter starts his October 14 letter by repeating his request – in stronger terms – that Myrtle stop using V-Mail to write him when he is at 'Camp.' He alludes to a problem with V-Mail but never explains its nature.

Marine protocol governing correspondence has become even more rigid. Now, in addition to not being able to reveal his location, he is also required to close with his full name and rating: 'Walter Erwin Dodd PhM1/c USNR.'

He has been out of the office and in the field for a few days. "It was a swell vacation for me & enjoyed it a great deal. This time I fired a B.A.R. for the first time. Guess I'll stick to the carbine or M-1. Only hit 2 surprise targets out of ten shooting offhand. I'm sending along a couple money orders with this letter…. There is a package slip here so will go down tomorrow & see what you sent."

He has seen a number of movies and was not impressed. He has received a note from Violet Davis and seems concerned about her. Walter's letters from 1943 mentioned that Mr. Davis was very ill, but now it appears Mr. Davis has died. "She must be very much upset yet. Guess she is still living in their place. Just wonder what she will do because I'm sure she can't live alone." The Davises were very good to Walter, taking him in over the Christmas holiday and truly treating him like family.

"Our new regimental surgeon is going to start a school for PhMs. It's a good idea if they really go at it and try to teach us something." I wonder how many of the corpsmen besides Walter are interested in going back to school. Since he has to be there, I think he wants to do the best work possible.

Walter begins his next letter with a small change. His location, which he has previously labeled simply as 'Camp,' has become 'Base Camp.' It seems unlikely that they have actually moved to another camp. Like the decree that letters must close with the writer's full name, it is hard to see how this change could serve any purpose. Nevertheless, Walter maintains it on subsequent letters.

"October 19, 1944 -Dear Folks, I'll write this note on the 4th Marines' latest job of publicity." He refers here to the new, official, Marine letterhead. In addition to the Marine emblem showing eagle, globe, and anchor, it now has three blood red stars - labeled 'Roi-Namur, Saipan and Tinian.'

After he acknowledges receiving Myrtle's packages and letters, Walter writes, "Likely by now Dad is home again & the next letter will tell me about it." Something, family, or business, has drawn Pop away from the ranch. Walter does not say, and I am mystified. In the nearly twenty years I lived on the ranch, Pop generally went to town once a week and in all those years never stayed away overnight. David comes to the rescue again, in an e-mail. "I remember Pop was gone when his brother died in WA and he flew there for the funeral. He was only gone a few days."

Although the medical classes Walter mentioned have begun, he writes, "So far they haven't conducted a class that has been coherent but maybe will get organized later on." Since his time in combat, Walter has neglected military minutia such as haircuts, and uniforms. "Went to town yesterday …. Had a rate sewed on my shirt. It's the first 1/c that I have worn although I've had the rate since May." Walter mentions Zaar and

Munski frequently, and it is clear he has grown genuinely fond of them. He will continue to risk everything to protect them when they return to combat.

October 24, he writes again. For this letter he has cut and pasted the new emblem onto regular sized onion skin paper. "This has been a very pleasant day for a change - a liberty day too. The truck ride into town is far too rugged for the amount of pleasure we usually have." He does not explain why this day is better than any other. He thanks Myrtle for his birthday present, a box of fruit, and writes, "I would like to have a picture of you to see how you look with your new teeth. How do they feel?"

His reservations about the new training seem to have disappeared. "I'm sure I didn't mention the lab class. The PhM1/c is very good & is an instructor as well. Now I'm learning the parts of the microscope & the reasons for doing some of the things I used to do. The minor surgery may develop well soon. Dr Baker ... is good, occasionally gives us a small lecture when we bring up some questions." This is typical of Walter. Given a worthwhile goal – such as improving his medical knowledge or skill – he works hard and is satisfied.

"My hearing has greatly improved since returning from combat. When I first came back it was terrible, but now, I can hear most of what goes on.... Love, Walter. Walter Erwin Dodd PhM1/c USNR."

On October 29th Walter closes out the month with a note to Byron who will turn 21 the following day. "Wish I was there to properly celebrate the day. David could no doubt hold you while I took care of the rest." The obligatory birthday spanking, a form of rough brotherly affection no longer in vogue today, was the norm in 1944.

Walter then adopts a serious tone. "Read that the restriction was being lifted on ammunition; were you able to get much .22 caliber this past summer? Guess pretty soon the coyote hides will be getting prime. This note is a bit late but sent with best wishes. Your brother, Walter."

When Walter writes on November 4, he has opened all his own birthday presents. He has received candy, a travel razor and 'Pathfinder,' an inspirational news magazine focusing on the war.

His favorite gift is from Myrtle. "…so glad to find it was this particular type of ring. Not so long ago I nearly bought a USN ring but those have such large tops I didn't like them. This is swell – now I'll get rid of this Jap ring I've been wearing." He does not describe the ring further except to call it "a perfect fit".

Besides preserving his 314 war-time letters, Walter also left a large rolltop desk crammed with items of all sorts. I have kept the desk and most of this memorabilia and after reading this letter I open a drawer and retrieve a small, faded, cardboard box. The ring inside is gold colored, and the top, which is stamped with an anchor embossed with the letters 'USN,' is indeed quite large. Each shoulder is embossed with an eagle bearing a shield. This ring has been worn and the band shows several dings, as though it has been caught, perhaps between a rock and a hard place. Engraved inside the band I can make out 'WED.' I slip the ring on. It is too large, and I wipe it off and return it to the box.

Walter reviews some recent movies, which I'm sure Al and Myrtle have not seen, and shares a military anecdote. "Chief Cochrane told me that the fellows in this Division's chief section were a very funny assortment of men. Yesterday there was a meeting & he wasn't interested to go so sent me in his place – now I agree completely with him.

"Mother, I want to wish you the best of everything on your birthday. I'll be thinking of you. Love, Walter." His letter will likely still be in transit when Pop collects their mail on Friday, November 10, two days before her birthday.

"Base Camp November 6, Dear Folks…. Today we got a new Remington typewriter – our old one is pretty well shot but it's still better than the war production model. Wouldn't work at first. The Battalion furnished a free beer party & it was compulsory for all to attend." Walter was perhaps the only reluctant guest. "You can bet it's noisy around here now."

Walter describes an inspection…. "The corpsmen really went to town on the job of cleaning sick bay – white washed the walls, oiled the deck & had the furniture painted. The surprising part was that the Old Boy complimented us on it. Tomorrow is election. Maybe we'll listen to the results. Love, Walter."

Walter's November 11 letter is a mix of news from family and the Corps: Births, illnesses, and memories from the first, and braggadocio, meals, and medals from the second. "Yesterday was the Marine Corps 169th anniversary so they sent around special messages that would make Hitler look like a piker & of course a couple good meals. Then the purple hearts were awarded.

"I notice that the order has come to discontinue using money stamped 'Hawaii' in the Pacific. Guess they don't believe the Japs are going to capture any more land.... Love, Walter."

November 14, just three days later Walter has three new letters from Myrtle to answer. Her letters seem to arrive in clumps, and I can see why. They still have no home mail delivery, so Walter's letters all end up at the Missoula post office twelve miles from the ranch. Typically, every Friday Pop makes his weekly trip to town. First, he drops off the cream at Community Creamery and the eggs at Stop and Shop before swinging by the post office where he mails any letters and opens Box 618. While Pop's trips are as regular as cows and chickens, weather delays and other factors make mail delivery sporadic.

Walter is busy with paperwork. "Entering the awards in the records is going to be a big job because we can't find a Purple Heart Stamp to use & I will have to write it all in by hand.... All but three of the corpsmen have been recommended for some special award.... They put me down for the Silver Star and also the Bronze Star. I'll be satisfied if I can come home in one piece." The two recommendations Walter refers to may be for the same incident.

"Boy, this tent could go into business & sell shaving cream, powder etc. I received 2 more boxes. They say there's a good show on tonight & that we should go, hate to go in the rain. Love, Walter." The tent, which Walter likely shared with two or three other corpsmen, was almost certainly a wall tent, sixteen-foot square, and made of heavy, water resistant canvas.

Base Camp Nov 18, 1944. Walter begins with a little harmless gossip – letters he has sent and received, how fast his brothers are growing up, and then, perhaps thinking of Christmas, remarks, "Guess I'll keep this pay check, just might have use for a bit of it."

As their next assignment approaches, Walter admits, "We all wonder what our new corpsmen will act like in combat. Certainly getting a bunch of Jews in & then we call Zaar 'rabbi.' He is Swedish & English but sort of fits him in some ways. Wish we had more like him though."

He sets the letter aside for two days and begins again. "We've had a very busy time. We gave the battalion a couple shots as they came thru the pay line…. I hear we have about seven more coming." Immunization boosters sometimes produce a reaction. Catching the men as they line up for pay is an almost sure-fire way to inoculate the reluctant.

"I've got some forms in now so I can get the health records in order. Do believe they are in good shape except a couple of boys have changed their home address…. Love, Walter E. Dodd PhM1/c USNR."

On November 27, for the first time in months, Walter types a letter. "Dear Folks since I'm down here in the office I'll try using this little portable machine. Every time I use it, I get so mad because it very often types two or three times in the same place."

Walter is back to pushing paper full time. "We have to make out a card on every man in the Battalion with his religion and next of kin. With the help of two other fellows I did a company and a half one day, takes quite a while.

"Doggone, but when Byron gets wound up, he can certainly write a letter. It would be very nice to see that horse, Guy, that he kept raving about. He didn't say a thing about Maggie, though." Walter may intend this as a joke. Maggie was a large, lazy, black, mare. Like Nellie, she enjoyed walking under low branches, in the hope of unhorsing the unwary.

Walter is still interested in submarines. Two months ago he considered transferring to submarine school, but never quite did. Now he has met "… a fellow over here on leave who is a gunner's mate aboard a submarine…. He has been around Japan several times and has taken pictures. He has told us about several of the secret instruments aboard.

Now I would like to go aboard and see some of the things. Plan to do so next time I have a chance.

"Nearly forgot to tell you but we did have a good thanksgiving dinner, but they didn't have any cranberry sauce. Is it hard to get this year I wonder?

"About enough for one night so will close. Love, Walter E. Dodd PhM1/c."

In his letter of December 2, he thanks Myrtle for her letter and a roll of film, and then launches into a stream-of-consciousness monologue describing the day's events.

He relates another rumor that is making the rounds, "Just heard today that all of us were cracked up or killed. One of the fellows who joined us shortly before we left last time got scared, returned to the beach & was evacuated. He spread that word to some of the fellows back there.

"We got quite a kick out of Thomas this morning when he had sick bay watch. He is noted for his plain and plentiful speech, but this was something." When it was necessary to shut down the sick bay temporarily, "…Thomas sent the men away with a 'Hoist anchor and shove off.' Very definite, don't you think?

"Some of our boys were caught again. An old service saying -very true - 'it isn't what you do but what you get caught doing' sort of applies here. Munski, Hearn & Baker were caught by the major drinking beer in the tent at 0900 this morning, gave them two weeks restriction. Ironically, Munski wasn't even drinking but was in the tent so was guilty too."

Switching to events back home, Walter continues, "That hunting trip sounded very simple. Wonder how Byron would tell it? Why didn't he use the Chevrolet? Bet my old wreck of a Chevy truck would have made it. Went up there many times before." Walter cannot resist the slight dig at Byron. "How is David making out this year? Love Walter E. Dodd PhM1/c USNR."

This is the first time since the Marines shoved off for Saipan that Walter has shown this much interest in events back home. Even so, his question about David reads like an afterthought. The ranch is nearly two years and 3,000 miles away. Letters have become Walter's only link to home. By day he pushes piles of paper. He lives in a tent on a tropical isle and writes letters that must pass the censor's stamp. Except for 'the boys' he is alone. His friends now are other corpsmen, and his brothers are Munski, Zaar, DeVore and yes, even men like Hearn.

By the end of December 1944, he will finish his 275th letter to the 'Folks.' Counting the hundreds of other letters to his numerous cousins, aunts, uncles, and neighbors, he must have written thousands. I do not count his 'hard letters' to the parents of corpsmen killed on Saipan or Tinian. Numerically they don't amount to much, but they take their toll, even invading his dreams.

On December 7, he writes, "Well the boys settled the argument of how to spell 'interpretation.' Munski checked the dictionary in sick bay." In this letter Walter never mentions ranch or family. He has reasons - paperwork, a fever from one of his immunizations, a large military award ceremony. Ever polite, he thanks Myrtle for the fruitcake (again) and for the roll of film he has just received, and comments, "I really got a kick out of your interpretation of the 'beer party'.

"Received a letter from one of our corpsmen in the states giving us some dope on what happened to some of our gold bricks & misfits. It certainly hurts to see these fellows get good duty simply by refusing to do their job over here." This is apparently the same fellow who refused to go ashore on the landing and was subsequently evacuated. Walter continues, "This bum says that we all either cracked up or were killed. About the fourth day on Saipan looked to me like it was going to be to the last man all right. Wish we could expect better treatment next time. Love, Walter E, Dodd."

To Walter, the 'bum' has abandoned his fellows, besmirched their good name, and is now lying about it. Walter has no sympathy for a man who fails his friends.

"Base Camp Dec. 15. Dear folks, guess you've been wondering why I haven't written, no particular reason." Walter continues for two pages without saying much. He saw a movie about Saipan and was disappointed. He has been issued a new rifle which is okay but not as good as the old one. The weather is cold and wet. "Will answer some of your questions next time. Love, Walter E. Dodd."

Like his previous one, Walter's letter of December 18 is devoted almost exclusively to base camp news. He confesses to becoming "... a terrible movie hound." He also describes a corpsman's party "... at a doctor's cabin on the beach with steaks & 20 cases of beer. Not bad." Walter is not a beer drinker, even though he may have tasted it - just to make sure.

He mentions two corpsmen who were reduced in rank "... because they didn't check out on liberty & were late checking in & brought in by the MPs. They were charged with AWOL for over 10 hrs. "Dr. Baker was transferred from this outfit 12-13-44. I was very sorry to see him go but we can't begrudge him some good duty.... Love, Walter E. Dodd."

About this time the folks would also have received a most unusual card. Sized especially for V-Mail and designed to do double duty this card bears these words in block print, "4Th MARINE DIVISION - MERRY CHRISTMAS - HAPPY NEW YEAR." It depicts a chubby, white-bearded fellow, dressed as Santa, except for the battle helmet, bearing a carbine and sitting atop a globe of the earth. Perched on his right shoulder and looking at him in apparent consternation, is the Marine eagle. "Santa" is slumped forward and may be passed out, perhaps from strong drink. Internet searches for images of this card have proved fruitless, but the postmark and Walter's signature on the lower right corner cannot be denied.

The third sentence in Walter's next letter, written on Christmas day, lends credence to my 'drunken Santa Claus' speculation. "Some of the fellows have sort of gotten into the mood with the aid of considerable spirits – heard them all night."

Despite having his rest interrupted, Walter strikes a cheerful note. "We had a good meal but no cranberry sauce. These last two days have been beautiful. Hope you have been experiencing the same sort of weather." Walter describes a trip he took with Munski and his brother. They went to "... the top of the mountain. Certainly enjoyed getting up where I could get a lung-full of air." The 'mountain,' Haleakala, is a dormant volcano that tops out at over 10,000 feet. Winter can bring snow, and freezing temperatures on the summit, perhaps reminding Walter of Montana.

As their departure approaches, Walter predicts, "No doubt the next few days I'll be very busy in the office as it's the end of the month and the quarter also." Personal matters occupy him as well. "I'm going to enclose a couple money orders and perhaps the pen Dan sent me, probably will enclose the box for my ring." His mood continues to shift. "We had a corpsman, a Jew, that the fellows liked, but like a lot of good men he was killed. He had just received word that his wife had a son a couple days before he was killed."

Walter closes with the hope that "…it will be possible to spend Christmas together not too many years from now – if only it could be next time. My best wishes are with you for the coming year. Love, Walter."

Late New Year's Eve, Walter closes the year with a three page letter. His description of the Marine's awards presentation fills a page. He writes, "…we marched to the usual area & 170 officers & enlisted men go down & are decorated in front of the Regiment ranging from the Navy Cross to the Bronze Star." Walter was nominated for a Silver Star but received a certificate for a Bronze instead. "The medal will be sent some time later as they had only about 1/3 enough for the occasion. Munski was recommended for the S.S. but his was boosted to the Legion of Merit. It is really nice to see him get it." The Legion of Merit actually ranks just below the Silver Star, so Walter's remark leaves me confused.

Perhaps these statements reveal Walter's true feelings about awards in general, "The only thing medals are presented for is for the morale of the rest of the boys. Of course, none of the fellows who received them were doing it for the purpose of the medal, but looks nice for the fellows going in." As to his own award, he cautions Myrtle, writing, "Don't let Mrs. Pope get any ideas about the thing." Walter knows that their neighbor, Mrs. Pope, is a tireless booster who would promote Walter as a 'war hero' given any encouragement, something he does not want. At this point Walter pauses his letter and goes to collect his pay.

When he returns, he has a patient, who "… got into a fight & fell on a tent peg, then when he came to, he went to the shower room & passed out. He crawled to sick bay or towards it & someone helped him. Wish Dr. Porter were there to look at him."

Walter asks Myrtle to use airmail for a while because other mail is so slow. Picture taking continues to be a problem. After finally obtaining a camera, film was scarce, then there was no paper for prints, and now "… only official cameras are allowed in the Division, too bad…. Love, Walter."

January 7, 1945, and Walter is marking time. With the holidays over, he seems more relaxed and there is less to do so he can catch up on his letters, read, and try to enjoy his few remaining weeks before shipping out. He manages to crack a few jokes. On receiving a letter from Bill Vetter, a neighbor known for his windy, discombobulated speech, Walter notes, "Bill writes just like he talks & wanders around as much."

He adds a story about Saipan. "Just talking to a fellow that was in the platoon, already a lot of the things we did are a little funny now – but were desperate at the time. He was a machine gunner during the operation & on top of carrying the gun & ammunition, carried a sledge hammer to break the rocks in the fox hole – It used to be enough to make a person swear & at times almost cry when we would run into a big rock right in the middle of the hole & be far too tired to start over again. We can bear to think of it now."

For whatever reason, Walter is opening up, sharing more information with Myrtle about his combat experiences. Though he presents them lightly, I wonder how much she worries.

As the Division readies itself for the next assault, carousing reaches new heights. "Gee, the extent some of these fellows go in gambling. The other night I hear a man lost $1,900 in one night, mostly dice I guess…. Baker amused me; he received a letter from his mother telling him to go easy on the beer. He was trying to figure who told her he was drinking too much because he'd been 'very careful' of what he wrote. He used to brag that she understood him very well & I guess she's better at it than he supposed. Love, Walter."

"January 10, 1945. Dear Folks, received 2 more letters last night from you – one really from Byron & what a letter it is. Certainly, he should do fine when it comes to an essay in school as far as length. Believe I should go back and count the words."

Perhaps in response to a question from Myrtle, he writes, "Don't believe one can forecast weather here – at least I can't. Pretty apt to have all of it every day anyway.

"I see the Chief bought a couple good books, 'Brave Men' by Ernie Pyle & 'Saratoga Trunk.' Have read several books, one-a-day for a change." Walter never mentions his current duties, but if he has time to read a book a day, they must be minimal.

"Oh yes, sounds like you might be exaggerating some things far too much. Medals are given for the morale of new fellows. Also most of the write-up that goes with them." Walter is typically modest, but from what I know of his actions in combat, Myrtle may not have been exaggerating at all.

On January 16, in a V-Mail, he tells Myrtle he got her letter, his khaki needs laundering, and his watch gains 2 minutes a week. The truest line in the letter is this one: "Haven't very much to say."

On January 21, he writes a wonderful letter to brother David. "Dear David, when are you going to send me a picture of your little dog?... What kind of a garden will you have from that seed you sent for? Have you a place of your own to plant it? .... Those are swell grades you received.... Sounds to me you like the teacher this year. I guess you know you got me in a lot of trouble when you gave the teacher my address... I will write to your friends soon. Your brother, Walter" David recalls that his teacher had every student write a letter to Corpsman Dodd. Now Walter feels obliged to answer them all.

The same day, Walter also writes to the folks and his main topic is mail. "I have about six letters here from you, some regular mail from way back & this month's air mail.... All the letters from the kids to answer. Bet the doctor *(censor)* will be as tired of reading them as I will trying to find something to say.... Have a letter from DeVore & pictures of his wife I'll send next time.... From an old letter sounds like you all had a nice Christmas – I'm glad.... I heard from Violet about 5 or 6 days ago & she sounded pretty good.... Guess I've about run down for this time. Love, Walter."

January 26 and Walter opens with, "I believe you must write more letters than I because I always seem to have several to answer, now 2 air mail & a regular.... I've enjoyed my last two liberties more than any for a long time. I saw a friend I knew at PSNY (Bremerton) & he told me about an officer we knew. I went & saw him too & he showed me around a bit. He certainly tickled me because he's the same as ever.... Can think of nothing more to say so will say goodbye. Love, Walter."

Walter's reunion with the fellows from Bremerton must have been bittersweet. His time serving at the Puget Sound Naval Yard hospital was his best duty. He made good friends, learned a lot from doctors he liked and respected, and acquainted himself with Seattle and the surrounding area. His regular visits to Marymoor Dairy Farm, which was managed by two of his uncles, allowed him to stay connected with his family. Marymoor was a first-class operation with modern machinery and practices, making it much superior to his folks' ranch in Montana.

When he left Bremerton in February of 1943 and entered the world of the Marines, Walter found a lot to dislike. It was as if all the flaws of the sailors - their drinking, cursing, whoring, fighting, and gambling – were multiplied. At various times, Walter has portrayed Marines as bums, braggarts, and thieves. He saw them as a brutal, rough bunch, and not very intelligent. Although the Marines have remained the same, Walter's perception of them has not. He has come to see Marines as tough and determined. Many are quite capable, and most are loyal to each other.

Throughout 1944, on Roi-Namur, Saipan, and Tinian, Walter saw and touched the bodies of dead Americans and Japanese. On Roi-Namur, he dragged hundreds of dead Japanese solders into mass graves. On Saipan, in addition to all the horrors of battle, he probably watched as thousands of terrified civilians leapt to their death from the island's cliffs. A week afterward on Tinian, he earned a nomination for the Silver Star for his heroic rescue of wounded Marines while under heavy enemy fire. Periodically deafened by artillery fire, he cared for wounded Marines during all three assaults. Obviously, these events changed his perspective. Many of the Marines are heartbreakingly young, and to Walter they have become "the boys."

Now, on February 2, 1945, a year after the assault on Roi-Namur, Walter writes from aboard ship on his way to Iwo Jima. "Dear Folks, As I wrote the date, I realized that this is 'ground hogs' day there, but of course here it could hardly have any significance.... We're allowed to say we're aboard ship & going into combat, but this letter will be delayed.

"So far, I have fared pretty well, only sick a couple days. Today I'll fire my shotgun for the first time just to see if it works.... Now things have settled down to the routine of trying to keep clean on a very limited amount of water.... Someone, for the benefit of the daily newspaper, figured that if everyone took a shower every day, we would each have 40 seconds under the shower."

On a morbid but realistic note, he adds, "Noticed a mimeographed letter in the chaplain's office for fellows to send home but the only thing that might be of use is my service no – 660-10-78." If for some reason a Marine suddenly stopped writing home, a service number would allow a family to make further inquiries. Of course when a Marine was killed in action the family was notified, nearly always, by telegram.

Although maintaining secrecy about their mission has become moot – the 'operation' will be nearly over before his letter is delivered – Walter is carefully vague about geography, writing, "...that mountain that we spoke of some time back, I can tell you something about it.... Boy, this old tub has been rolling the past two days. Things certainly have to be lashed down now.... Well we've been schooled on the place we're to hit. No. of troops, size of place & just about everything except who isn't going to get hurt.... Today is also an anniversary for the Fourth Div. Remember where we were a year ago?" Walter remembers that one year ago to the day he was on Namur when Japanese soldiers launched their last, futile counterattack. The battle for Roi-Namur lasted less than a week, and he expects the fight for Iwo Jima to last longer and result in more casualties. He knows that to acknowledge this fact would only worry Myrtle.

On February 4 he adds a short post script. "My shotgun works OK & not too much recoil so guess I'll carry it in. Not much else to say now so if things go well, I'll write after the operation. Love, Walter."

On February 12, aboard ship approaching Tinian, Walter writes a short note. Tomorrow a 'rehearsal' is scheduled and on the 16th the fleet will sail for Iwo Jima. "Dear Folks, received a letter from you dated Jan. 27… I am not attempting to answer any letters now but will after the operation, nothing to say & anyway they won't go thru for some time. Love, Walter." He will not write again for two weeks.

Marine records show the Fourth Division departing Hawaii on January 27 and heading for Iwo Jima. According to Walter, a letter written in Montana and dated January 27 was delivered to him aboard ship in the Pacific on February 12. Research reveals that mail went by fixed wing planes to Aircraft Carriers while in transit and was then delivered among the vessels in the group.

When Walter writes on February 27, he has been on Iwo Jima for about a week. "Dear Folks, just a line to let you know I'm still OK. So far have been very lucky and terribly tired. Today is our second day of rest so I can almost walk without too much effort. We're in an anti-mine trap right now, watching the stuff go both ways. Just had an anniversary on Feb. 26 - two years with the Marines. Hardly anything to celebrate but there was quite a display here on Iwo then. Found a .45 automatic on the lines a few days ago so have never carried the shotgun, haven't even fired the thing yet. You know it felt cold to us here but we're getting a little used to it now. Love, Walter."

What is an 'anti-mine trap'? I can find no reference, but it sounds a bit like a foxhole only larger, though if that is so, why not call it one? Walter is so exhausted he can only watch 'the stuff go both ways.' I try to visualize him, along with several other corpsmen, lying exhausted in a depression, perhaps bordered by a few sandbags, a couple hundred yards behind and to the side of the Marine lines, watching tracer rounds as the Marines and Japanese exchange fire.

For five days Walter has been tending wounded Marines. When he left the landing craft and struggled ashore, the beach was still being raked by Japanese machine gun fire. He passed the bodies of uncounted Marines. He gives no details in his letter, but he has undoubtedly dealt with torn flesh, broken bones, crushed skulls, gaping internal wounds, severed limbs, and lots of blood.

Before the battle American military planners felt that Iwo Jima could be taken in 4 to 7 days with moderate Marine casualties. The planners were disastrously wrong. The battle for Iwo Jima took 36 days, resulted in the deaths of 7,000 Marines and 19,000 Japanese, and left 19,000 Marines wounded. For the Marines, the battle was the costliest of the war.

There are several reasons why Iwo Jima was so much more difficult than Tinian and even surpassed Saipan. Throughout 1944, the commander, General Kuribayashi, had heavily fortified the island's bunkers and tunnels, making them more resistant to artillery and air attack. Also, the general had changed his tactics since Saipan and Tinian. There Japanese defenders revealed their positions too soon and were decimated by artillery and bombs. On Iwo Jima, the defenders waited almost an hour after the Marines landed before opening up with all their weapons for devastating effect. Finally, the Marines had been told that walking up the beaches was 'easy.' In reality, once off the relatively narrow beaches they were confronted by 15-foot, 45-degree slopes composed of soft, volcanic ash that stopped the advance of the Amtracs and even impeded the tanks. Reporter Robert Sherrod, who was imbedded with the Marines on Iwo Jima, called it "a nightmare in hell."

Unlike Sherrod, Walter is writing for a small audience and tries hard not to alarm the Folks. He even attempts nonchalance by pointing out his two year anniversary was marked by "quite a display."

Now that he can "almost walk without too much effort" it is probably time for him to go back to work. Some of the worst fighting is yet to come.

"March 11, 1945, Dear Folks, The Corps have furnished each of us with a pad of paper so there is little or no excuse for not writing. Well we went into reserve yesterday. Such a relief from the eighth which I believe was our worst day. Seems that the casualties were so badly shot up or serious that it has been terrible."

Walter writes this one week after the action in which he earned his second Bronze Star. According to the commendation the award was "For heroic achievement … on March 4, 1945, when enemy fire had thwarted all attempts to rescue a wounded Marine…Dodd, completely disregarding his own safety, entered the enemy's line of fire, led his party to the wounded and directed the evacuation without further injury." The citation goes on but as Walter points out elsewhere, medals don't necessarily tell the real story.

Many years later, when he was in his nineties Dad gave me his recollection of what I believe is the same event. As Walter recalled, he had taken Hearn and two other corpsmen to pick up two wounded Marines from the front lines. To get back to a sheltered area they had to cross a field covered by an enemy machine gunner. The first two corpsmen carried one Marine to safety with no problem. Walter and Hearn prepared to follow with the second Marine. As Walter recalled, "Hearn had the front of the stretcher. We had just started moving when the Jap machine gunner opened up behind us. Hern was a big sloppy guy and he sort of bounced when he ran. I could see the tracers, and they were getting closer, so I yelled at him, 'Faster Hearn, he's gaining on us!' You should have seen that fat man run! I was laughing so hard I could barely keep up." Dad told this story more than once and the phrase "You should have seen that fat man run!" was always the punch line. Walter told me with what sounded like pride, that no corpsman was ever killed or seriously injured while picking up the wounded under his direction.

Walter's March 4, letter continues. "It will be over very soon now. So far, I have no souvenirs but feel very fortunate to be here yet. Erwin & I have one of the deeper foxholes here in the side of the hill. As bad as this operation has been, we corpsmen have had plenty of food, water, & sleep. We've had to stand very little security guard.

"At first we had to carry litters over very rough ground & down a cliff but the period after our first rest we started using the ambulance. I strained my back on the first part & was very painful. Last night it didn't hurt for the first time…. Don't believe I'll write again before I leave here. Maybe I won't write until we get back to Camp. Love, Walter. Walter E. Dodd PhM1/c USNR."

Walter's next letter is from Maui on April 6. "Dear Folks, you can't imagine how happy we are to be back here at our old rest camp. The trip coming back has seemed so long & longer still for me because I was really sea sick for the first half of it. We were really surprised at the reception that the folks here gave us. It seemed sincere & was very welcome. Guess we're just all very glad to be alive. This is going to be strictly a war edition and won't attempt to answer your letters until I'm sort of caught up on them. There is a whole stack of them here.

"Sort of made me sore today when we came in, the first thing they asked for was a list of men who rated the Purple Heart. Since none of the company offices are open, we can't be very thorough, but we sent a list such as it was.

"Did you notice, the Marines are keeping the stationary right up to date?" On April 6, the day Walter arrives on Maui, the Fourth Division has already updated its gaudy, three-color-onion-skin stationary, which is now emblazoned with Roi-Namur, Saipan, Tinian, and Iwo Jima.

Walter is sharing a four-man tent with Munski, another corpsman, and the chief. "The chief has been playing his phonograph every day. One of the nicest things I've heard in a long time. We had a swell chaplain aboard ship & he played the phonograph there, but I didn't care so much for the selections."

Erwin, the corpsman Walter shared a foxhole with on Iwo Jima, "… got some bad news, upon his return, his fiancé has been married for about 2 months & hasn't told him yet. He wondered why he wasn't hearing from her. It happens to so many.

"Most of the fellows are drunk tonight & will probably remain so for 3 days." I am struck by Walter's empathy and his priorities. He has been through the same ordeal as 'the fellows' who are on a three-day bender, yet he does not fault them or begrudge them their spree. Instead he sets to reading and answering the pile of letters waiting for him.

"Base Camp, April 14, 1945 – Dear Folks, the rumor is very strong that we (corpsmen only) may go stateside as soon as we complete our 18 months over here. We can hope & do."

By July 8, Walter will have been in the Pacific for 18 months. At that point he will have been on Maui for about a year, spent over three months aboard ship, and seen nearly three months of action on Roi-Namur, Saipan, Tinian, and Iwo Jima.

In the meantime, Walter's only immediate duties appear to be a bit of Navy paperwork and a lot of personal correspondence. He continues with, "I have 12 letters here from you... Saturday E. Post is coming thru... Mother the cookies arrived but were rather old tasting, too bad because they must have been good... we have a wonderful NCO club... breakfast, always juice...a surprise & a pleasure."

"Doctors Porter and Lyon came through okay... There are three of us corpsmen who don't have the Purple Heart now. I could have gotten it this time if I'd put in for it.

"We have received the sad news of the President's death. Just wonder how our new president will make out. Wish it were somebody else....

"Must write to Violet. Also, I'm going to try to read & relax tomorrow. Probably end up working though.... Sending a little Jap currency. Love, Walter."

The next day, April 15, he writes to David. "You haven't said anything about doing any horseback riding or milking cows – What have you been doing? We have so many new fellows I sort of feel out of place. Think maybe I'd better come home, don't you? Your brother, Walter."

"April 21, Dear Folks, gee it would be nice to be back there now at this time of year instead of wasting my time here punching a typewriter. Boy am I having a terrible time closing out the service records of the boys killed in action. The paymaster is obstinate & now the company commander doesn't want to sign. Guess I'll try once more & then don't know, just send it in unsigned. They don't find anything wrong just don't feel that they should sign that particular page."

Walter says no more about Iwo Jima. Instead he reviews the local entertainment and sets the letter aside. The next day, he fills two pages.

"The Chief and I went horseback riding.... I had a small bay that was very good but didn't get silly. If we go again think I'll try a big sorrel."

While the Marines and Corpsmen continue to party, Walter writes, "April 27, ... glad to hear you are getting my letters, not that there is much to write about. Boy are we having an argument, on all subjects – the peace, Truman, Wheeler, just everything." Walter doesn't mind the arguments and even appears to relish them. They may keep his thoughts from dwelling on the horrors he has seen and cannot forget.

"Believe I'll just let the money stay in the bank for a while. If I come home, we'll see about it then, if not." Myrtle has been banking his pay, and his "If I come home" remark acknowledges the fact that Japan is still refusing to surrender, even though they are losing badly.

May 4, 1945, "Dear Folks, this has been inspection day & this afternoon we were paid. Will send a couple money orders. Drew $325 this time... Mother I'm wishing you a swell day next Sunday which is Mother's Day. Love, Walter"

"Base camp May 11, 1945 .... Some of the boys seem to be quite confident that all the infantry corpsmen will be relieved, but I'll believe it when the orders come in.

"Dr. Porter received his (transfer) orders. I'd feel lost without him if we had to go into combat again because we've become so used to him." Porter has commanded the corpsmen beginning with Rio-Namur. His decorations include the Legion of Merit and two Bronze Stars. Long after the war, Walter spoke highly of Dr. Porter. "Dr. Owen replaced him. He seems very steady & conscientious, & I believe the boys will respect him in combat as well as here."

Even though Germany surrendered unconditionally on May 7, four days before his letter, Walter did not mention it and his comment about 'Dr Owen and combat' suggests to me that he believed the Marines would face further fighting, probably in Japan itself. Japan's only hope was to make the price of an American victory so great that the US would settle for less than an unconditional surrender. Indeed, the US Military's estimate of US losses resulting from a land invasion of Japan was between 400,000 and 800,000 US deaths. Sixty-five years later,

Walter told me that if such an invasion had occurred, he believed he would have been killed.

"Well Hearn is up for another court martial… for fighting with civilians." Hearn is a Texas boy with an attitude who drinks and fights. In his official picture we see him with his cap askew wearing a smirk. Hearn was present on all four assaults Roi-Namur, Saipan, Tinian, and Iwo Jima, and Walter is used to him by now.

Apparently, Myrtle has informed Walter of two potential post-war jobs. One is from their neighbors, the Popes, and Walter writes, "I'm sure it wouldn't interest me." The other, from Myrtle's sister Ruby, and her husband John, draws this reaction, "… it would be very interesting for say 6 months only but I'm sure I don't want to work for anyone too long."

Walter has been taking orders for over three years and though he is clearly tired of it, he manages an ironic joke. "Can't plan on anything yet & hope you don't either because you know (I do) I'm in the Marine Corps.

"Well the boys want me to get ready & go with them on a censorable, unauthorized trip so will close. Love, Walter." Walter will continue to do his duty for the Corps, but, like his mentors, Munski and DeVore, he understands that in day-to-day behavior, 'getting away with it' is what counts.

On May 16 he writes, "I'm getting quite restless; guess I've sort of outlived my time with this outfit. Certainly feel like the last leaf on a tree in the fall. Zaar, Erwin, & Flores have made PhM1/c on a recommendation from Dr Porter for outstanding work in the field. Certainly glad to see them make it, especially Zaar.

"Some new men just arrived. Boy has one fellow got a bad record. He has several Court Martials and was recommended once for a bad conduct discharge…. will bet a lot that he is never killed while attached here… a funny thing to say but would still bet on it."

In his May 26 letter, we learn that DeVore failed to 'get away with it' and "… has been busted to PhM2/c …. Guess his luck sort of ran out or they didn't think he was cute anymore…. He is on Okinawa now, but of course he has a good job, not up on the front lines."

On Maui, Walter notes, "'The Boys' are celebrating, probably another noisy night, liberty & all, and I see a couple bottles more – oh well our tent should be quiet, us old men. Love, Walter."

"May 31, Dear Folks .... I saw by the papers that yesterday was Memorial Day & noticed that the cemeteries are still decorated. They look pretty good today, but over here their cemeteries are usually in pretty poor condition."

Walter honored Memorial Day all his life. Every year when I was growing up, our family, led by Walter and Myrtle, would gather armloads of lilacs and whatever other fresh flowers we had. Then, rain or shine, busy with work or not, we would head for the cemeteries on Missoula's North side. I remember wandering behind as they placed flowers on the graves of family members.

"June 5, Dear Folks, no doubt it's time to drop another line, absolutely nothing to say, no rumors or anything.... We were supposed to have an area inspection by the commanding general but, I suppose due to weather conditions, he didn't show up.... Guess it is supper time so will close. Love to all, Walter."

"June 10, Dear Folks.... Rumors are starting to fly again. This time they say we will get our preparatory orders about June 13 for the first leg of our trip to the states. Really wouldn't surprise me though if they don't come till the first of next month.... Love, Walter."

"June 15, Dear Folks, well today I'm back in camp although wasn't due to return until Saturday but last night we had a patient, so I volunteered to bring him to the hospital. The doctor suggested I stay in & who am I to refuse a chance like that. I got to the tent about 0200 this A.M.

"How foolish of you folks to get excited about me coming home soon. First, we have to have replacements. I had never expected to get there before the first of Sept. These changes are very slow & have to go through many official channels." I take Walter's rebuke as evidence that Myrtle continues to pester him by speculating that his return is imminent. He is more than ready to be done with the Marines, and her overeager guesses must frustrate him. He switches to a somber subject.

"Tomorrow I must write a very hard letter in answer to one from a casualty's' folks. Have received another letter from Bill Nizzardi's sister. She had heard of the death of Marquez. Some time I hope to show you the letter she wrote to me when I sent the letter of condolence to his family. Certainly a painful thing to read when you realize the background. Would like to see Bill's mother sometime but she lives in Michigan. 'Nuff for now. Love, Walter."

This reference to Bill Nizzardi and Anthony Marquez requires an explanation. These two corpsmen, boys really, served with Walter in the First Battalion. They were PhM3/Cs and just 19 when they were killed. Nizzardi died eleven months before on Tinian, and Marquez has just died on Iwo Jima. Each received a Purple Heart and a Star – Silver for Nizzardi and Bronze for Marquez. When a man was killed the next of kin received a telegram, though sometimes a chaplain might write if the man was known to him. At least three times Walter has written letters to families himself. Among his files, I discover a draft of what I believe is his second letter to the Nizzardi family.

"Dear Mrs. Nizzardi & girls, I have read and reread your letter and believe that I can understand your feeling. Bill told me so much about you that I felt I knew you.... Apparently, our letters reached you before the Navy was able to notify you... I am sorry that the news reached you in this manner.

"Dr. Porter wrote you before and has written you again giving you most of the details you asked about. I was working with Bill that morning but was not with him the moment he was hit. He did a superb job that morning as he always did on anything he undertook.

"Like yourself I was almost sick and nearly lost faith in many things after that morning. There must be an explanation of why it should be he who was picked. Perhaps your Priest can find an answer." The next sentence is crossed out and illegible.

"Bill loved you all very dearly I know. For this reason, I'm sure he would want you to carry on as you would, were he coming back." More lines crossed out. "He was very proud that he had one sister who was leading a happy life, another the valedictorian of her class, and of his mother who loved to watch over the shop and youngsters who came there.

"If there is anything else you wish to know or anything that I or any of the corpsmen here can do please let me know because we will be more than glad to help." Walter does not sign the draft, but I imagine he closed his finished letter something like this - With the deepest sympathy, Walter E. Dodd PhM1/c.

Walter's letter of June 20 is short, light, and cheery as he rambles about memories of summer on the ranch, describes a Hawaiian afternoon liberty with Zaar, and closes with happy birthday wishes for David.

On June 26, Walter is in a darker mood. "We have no indication as yet that we will be relieved at all. After the second day on Saipan I really never figured that I would make it back in one piece until these last rumors started & then I did have a brief hope.... Received information on last corpsman who was wounded & evacuated from Iwo Jima, so now our records are straight ... until the next operation." Walter's reference to 'the next operation' is an ominous reminder that if Japan refuses to surrender, the Marines will likely be required to invade the Japanese homeland.

"June 29, Dear Folks, ... Frank (Munski) just came & told me I've another Bronze Star medal to be awarded.... Sort of too bad I should get two & some of these other boys didn't get any. Wonder what this was for? Oh well, it is always said by the boys that know, the medals don't mean much unless the true facts are known. I had intended to go into the field this time but guess I won't ask to because I'll want to get ready for the parade. It's going to be a huge ceremony this time. I was going out & try looking at some of the underwater life via the water goggles. They all say it's really a great thrill & one never tires of it because there is such a variety.... Will enclose a note to David. Love, Walter."

"June 29, Dear David, what is your job going to be in the hayfield this year? Do you suppose old Nellie would be safe for me to ride now? Bet it would be hard on me. Take care of things – your brother, Walter."

Walter writes again July 7. "This morning our parade was held, and decorations given... nearly 800 medals, mostly Bronze Stars.... I received the gold star." The Gold Star is in lieu of the second Bronze Star he earned on Iwo Jima, and he is not sure how to display it on his uniform.

"A general, receiving a Bronze Star, was in high spirits. He has about 14 ribbons so surely one more didn't matter unless he was working for a color scheme." Walter's sense of humor has become more sardonic. He sees the absurdity of 'serious' events, which to him, serve no good purpose.

"Probably you have a pretty good start on mowing by now. Wish I was there to help. I'm getting tired of this inactivity." With time to kill, and the persistent rumors predicting their imminent return to the states, Walter longs for the ranch.

He reassures Myrtle about their food. "We are getting fresh tomatoes & boy do I enjoy them. We have little to complain about at our mess." As to morale, "The drunks are beginning to show up. Lots of beer in camp today." He closes with optimism, "Should have some chocolate cake tonight. Love, Walter."

Just two days later, July 9, Walter writes again. He has no real news. Perhaps the most interesting part of the letter concerns language. "Boy, some of the fellows wonder what will happen when they get home and slip with the type of language they are accustomed to using over here. Some of the stuff that is said now would have floored these same fellows a couple years ago.... Enough for now – Love, Walter."

Walter, in the approximately 70 years I knew him, refrained from cursing or other vulgar speech. Just once, when I was about 19 and had driven my mother to tears – never mind why – Walter uttered a single 'Damn.' Remembering this today I am impressed and humbled.

On July 13 he writes, "Well some of us have just completed 18 months overseas today. Doesn't greatly matter I guess if we have to spend another 2 months with this outfit but I'm sure there are more pleasant places."

Walter has just seen the write-up for the Bronze Star he has received. "Don't believe there was much truth in the citation except the reference to continuous work." The citation includes the words tireless, courage and initiative, and the phrases 'heroic achievement,' 'highest traditions' and 'devotion to duty'." His modesty is honest though he does tend to underestimate himself.

The Corps is trying to entertain the men with movies, beer (naturally), and tonight a stage show with an all-Marine cast. Walter decides to take in the stage show and restarts his letter afterwards. "A swell show, the best we've seen in this camp. There are all kinds of ways to win the war I guess & these boys are doing their part.

"Just now remembered I was supposed to get something for the PR representative from our corpsmen who are to be decorated tomorrow. Will do it now. It's still a pretty poor risk for anyone to depend on my memory. More trouble about duplicate awards of PHM (purple hearts medals). Some are presented by FMF, Pac, Hospitals & here so we really get fouled up.

"July 16, Dear Folks, doggone seems like I've gotten into a sort of writing streak." Walter has not managed four letters in ten days since early in 1943, but he has seen what there is to see on Maui and his duties are extremely light.

Besides fixing up some health records, almost a make-work job, Walter has been watching Dr. Owen perform "… a couple minor procedures in Bn. (battalion) sick bay! First time I've seen it done under such conditions. Also aspirated a knee joint, been a long time since I've seen it done." Medicine on Iwo Jima was of the battlefield variety and Walter sounds pleased to renew his acquaintance with actual, non-emergency healing.

Walter includes with this letter a newspaper clipping dated July 11, headlined "Jap Admiral's Letter to Roosevelt Before Fall of Iwo Reported." The original story was written by New York Herald Tribune correspondent Emmet Crozier on April 4, 1945, so this subsequent article by another author is really third hand. Research in Wikipedia and US Naval records confirms that the letter was almost certainly written by Rear Admiral Toshi Ichimaru. It was found on the Admiral's body in a cave on Iwo Jima where he committed suicide shortly before the fall of the island's final defenses. The translation reads - "Though you may use the surprise attack on Pearl Harbor as … propaganda… I believe you know that you left Nippon no other method in order to save herself from self-destruction…. The white races, especially you Anglo-Saxons, at the sacrifice of the colored races, are monopolizing the fruits of the world…. The imperial majesty's true aim is no other than the attainment of everlasting peace."

Walter does not comment on the article, and we never spoke of it, so I don't know his thoughts. In high school I was given the standard story that the Japanese attack was completely unprovoked, and that December 7, 1941, was indeed 'a day of infamy.' Case closed.

In a bitter, rambling diatribe, the admiral argues that US economic policies forced Japan to attack Pearl Harbor. Americans dismissed this as nonsense until a group of 'revisionist' historians argued that the placing of embargos on the sale of copper and oil to Japan, was an American act of war. They pointed out that the US also froze all Japanese assets, another huge financial blow. I find the revisionist argument interesting but somewhat disingenuous. Because Japan had spent years establishing its own military empire over Manchuria, China, Korea, and the Philippines, I believe a military conflict with the US was already inevitable.

Walter ends his July 16 letter with news of the weather. "Feels sort of like a storm is brewing, glad I did my washing today. Sounds like some old housewife talking. Will close for now. Love, Walter."

"July 21, 1945 - Boy, have we been in a big argument about nothing, mostly about the disposition of these Pacific islands, of course the chief feels we should garrison all of them regardless of how many men it takes. Wonder how long he wants to stay in the service – or his children? This point system caused a lot of comment too. Of course, it doesn't apply to me; it would only take in fellows of about 40 years old or more."

This is the first time Walter mentions the point system, shorthand for the Adjusted Service Rating Score. The ASRC was created to clarify when "Uniformed Military individuals" became eligible for discharge. The intent was that those who had served longest and fought hardest, be the first sent home. To qualify for discharge, a man earned points based on four variables: time in service, months served overseas, combat awards received, and number of dependent children under eighteen. Arbitrary and rigid, this system caused immediate confusion, and modifications began at once.

To pass time, Walter attends movies, takes pictures, and listens to rumors. "We just got some scoop on the Cocoanut Grove fire in Boston.

(November 1942, over 400 deaths) It was this kid's first experience with the Marine Corps, a truckload of Marines drove up to the fire, picked up the cash register & left. He knows it wasn't turned over to proper authority because one of the privates in the truck was in his outfit & he got a cut out of it." This story sounds like the Marine version of an 'urban legend.' Records confirm that Marines assisted in the evacuation of some of the fire victims, but I can find no mention anywhere of a missing cash register or any alleged misbehavior by the Marines. As Walter observes, "A person can hear anything around here.... Love, Walter."

Walter writes the next Saturday, July 18. "I feel pretty tired... it was midnight before we got to bed. Washed all my dirty clothes – boy what a pile.

"Yesterday Munski & I each bought $150 worth of traveler's checks. Maybe it will be a little better than carrying the money." He has not mentioned shipping out, but this is an obvious signal.

"Tonight the NCO Club is passing out free beer & Coca Cola... Wish it were a steak dinner or something similar, beer is the most popular though. Think I may write again Tuesday. Love, Walter."

Besides the reference to traveler's checks, this letter contains another clue that Walter expects to return to the states soon. For almost two years, Walter has written "Walter E. Dodd PhM1/c" at the bottom of the last page of every letter – until this one. Perhaps the censor no longer cares.

Writing August 1, Walter's impatience shows. Without regular duties, he suffers through "...a terrible stage show... so lousy men made terrible cracks." As always, rumors remain rife: "Well we got word our orders are in but can't be sure until we see them. Will write again if it's true."

As he waits, he laments a lost opportunity. "Wish I had gotten to see Dr. Lyon play basketball. He was one of the best in college." Walter has lived and worked with these corpsmen and doctors for months. He will never see most of him after his discharge, though a few will remain lifelong friends.

He sets his letter aside. When he resumes later that day, he has more than rumor to report. "Just back from looking at the rough list of the draft to leave & see my name and also see Munski's on it too…. Guess I'll get packed tomorrow. Swell to get started again. Love. Walter E. Dodd."

By August 8th Walter is still waiting because "… they keep pushing up the date. The good thing about it though, it's a matter of days now instead of months…. Hope I get home for some good corn on the cob, haven't had any decent corn since I left home. We corpsmen have been having a lot of fun especially me because this is the first time since I was in old 'D' company back in Pendleton that I ever played around in the day & just loafed for over a day at a time."

Although Hiroshima was bombed August 6, the full story did not appear in many papers for a couple days, so it is a bit unclear exactly what Walter knew and when he learned it. He does write on August 8, "Will have to drop by the radio in about an hour & hear the president & then this evening will have to see what Japan has to say. Heard a newsflash from KNX last night that there would be an announcement of importance. Seems there can only be one thing for them to say now."

Walter holds the letter and on August 9th adds another page and a half. "Guess I was out in the sun a little too long as my arms are a little red…. Got a letter the other day that was very wet, guess they dropped a bag of mail in the ocean…. You'll find the gold star that was awarded in that big box coming to you, also my good pen…. I'll write again a time or two. Love, Walter." That evening Walter apparently learns that a second atomic bomb has just been dropped, this time on Nagasaki, and adds this postscript. "8-10-45 The news sounds very encouraging this A.M. Hope they make it unconditional. Walter"

By the time he writes again, nearly a week later, Japan has surrendered unconditionally. At the time Walter believed the two bombs had saved his life and the lives of tens of thousands other Marines. He held that opinion for the rest of his life.

"August 19, Dear Folks, I hadn't intended to write until I got to the States but since we're spending so much time fooling around decided to write a line. We aren't doing anything, although we rate liberty practically all the time…. Don't write to this place as the mail would only get sent around for a couple months. Love, Walter."

On August 23 he writes, "Dear Folks, I might as well keep you up to date …. We are still doing nothing…. First few days we were here we went all over the camp & into all the surrounding areas, then spent a few days at the recreation hut & read all the magazines, yesterday played cards all day so today went on liberty. I should bring something home for all of you but don't know what. All of this cheap junk sells for a terrific price. Probably go to Frisco & buy all kinds of Pacific junk much cheaper…. The way the boys around here are broke (financially) is terrific.

"From the news in the papers it seems that civilian life will be good again with all the gas, tires soon & the restrictions lifted on most other things. The only thing is there will be innumerable strikes all over now." Walter lodges a couple complaints – the water is "terrible" and the bed "too soft" – but they seem half-hearted. He closes with an admonition - "Do not write to me. Love, Walter E. Dodd PhM1/c"

Though this is his last letter, Walter's time in the service is not over. His comments reveal he is no longer on Maui, but still in Hawaii, perhaps Pearl Harbor. His Marine records show that a request for transfer to San Francisco, FFT, was submitted on 8/5/45, but not approved until 8/12/45. 'FFT,' in Navy jargon, translates to 'for further transport.'

PART 7 – WAITING FOR DISCHARGE – NO LETTERS
SEPTEMBER 1, 1945 – NOVEMBER 16, 1945

On September 1, 1945, six weeks after he wrote that "… another 2 months wouldn't matter much", Walter arrived in San Francisco. On September 4 he received written orders granting him thirty days leave with two days allowed for travel. He was instructed to find his own way home by train and, to "… not divulge any information whatsoever relative to the whereabouts or movements of any ships or any naval information to any unauthorized person. You will not participate in any press conference or talk to reporters or over the radio…. Failure to abide by the foregoing will render you liable to disciplinary action."

Walter's movements, thoughts and feelings over those forty-seven days are not recorded, but we can be sure he did not meet with the press. He probably spent most of his time at the ranch with Myrtle, Al, Byron, and David. He undoubtedly enjoyed a lot of Myrtle's cooking. There would have been fresh milk, home churned butter, eggs from Myrtle's hens and vegetables from her bountiful garden. He would have relished Myrtle's freshly butchered fryers as well as home smoked ham and bacon from their own pig. As David recalls, "Mother cut the meat up and cured it with brown sugar, and Pop put it on racks and kept the smokehouse going." Her bread, pies, and cookies – not off the boat but fresh from the oven – would have been his daily fare.

Walter's family, friends and neighbors would have flocked to see him while he was on leave. They would have been curious and surely asked many questions about the war. The Dodds and Chilcotes were great talkers, and in a group, they could raise quite a noise. Walter loved them all, but their questions would have disturbed him. He had been having horrible dreams – nightmares, really – for some time. They started not long after he first saw combat, and often interrupted his sleep.

Walter longed for quiet, which had been a rare commodity in the Navy. There, every day was filled with noise. Someone was always talking, arguing, yelling, or laughing. Aboard ship there was always the low rumbling thrum of the engines. The noise of combat was the worst of all because behind the clatter of small arms fire, the louder, ripping sound of machine guns, and the deafening booming impact of artillery shells, lay the screams and agonized moans of wounded, dying men. It was almost too much to bear, and even though it was over, the memories refused to leave his head.

Home at last, Walter found quiet in the woods. There, with a handsaw and an axe, he spent several days limbing deadfall that could be used as firewood. As he later recalled, "It was a great relief just to get away." There would have been no vehicle sounds, no planes in the sky, no human voices. There would have been bird sounds, the scolding chatter of a squirrel, and sometimes, if he paused and listened hard, the whisper of Butler Creek.

On October 6, when his leave was up, Walter reported as ordered to the Naval Recruiting Station in Helena. The Helena NRS extended his leave for fifteen days, and he returned to the ranch. His discharge was set for November 16, so after his extended leave he had only twenty-five days to serve. For all practical purposes Walter was of no further use to the Marines or Navy, but rules being rules, he would return to the Puget Sound Naval Hospital in Bremerton for those twenty-five days.

One might think Walter could travel by train directly from Missoula to Bremerton. Not so. The Navy required Walter to return to Helena, 115 miles east of Missoula, and there, early the morning of October 22, board a train for Seattle. This train, like all westbound trains, had to pass through Missoula, before proceeding to Seattle.

I'll ask David tell this part of the story. "The Northern Pacific Railroad tracks ran just across the highway from the DeSmet Grade School that I attended. Passenger trains always stopped on the double track there and waited for the single track to clear before proceeding. One evening as was normal, my father picked me up from school to take me back to our Butler Creek home. We had just left school and pulled out onto the highway. We saw someone leaning out the door of the train waving his arms. Pop stopped, got out and went over to the train. It happened to be Walter. They visited for several minutes until the line cleared and the train prepared to move on."

What were the odds? Perhaps about as good as Walter making it unscathed through the assaults on Roi-Namur, Saipan, Tinian, and Iwo Jima, except for a small piece of shrapnel in one arm.

After his overnight train ride, Walter reported as ordered to the Navy Barracks, Puget Sound Naval Yard, Bremerton, WA. There are no letters from Walter those final weeks. He was not immediately assigned any duties in Bremerton, so having learned from DeVore and Munski the fine art of avoiding work, he made himself scarce. "I just sort of flew under the radar," Walter explained seventy years later. He undoubtedly spent time at Marymoor farms, and perhaps looked up an old navy chief or two if they were still around.

On November 16, 1945, he received his NAVPERS-533, Notice of Separation from U.S. Naval Service. This one-page form reveals that Walter served in the Navy for 3 years, 10 months, and 15 days. He spent 14 weeks of that service in Medical Field Service Schools. The form also contains this list of Walter's medals: World War II Victory Medal, Good Conduct Medal, Presidential Unit Citation (1 star), American Area Campaign Medal, Asiatic Pacific Area Campaign Medal (3 stars), and Bronze Star Medal with Gold Star. The first Bronze Star was for Tinian, and the second, signified by the Gold star, for Iwo Jima.

Just above the list of medals, the insurance section shows that Walter intended to keep his Navy life insurance with its total monthly premium of $6.70 for two $5,000 policies. This section also shows Walter's 'total payment upon discharge' at $354.09. This includes the munificent sum of $100 for 'initial mustering out pay.' These figures raise questions; how much money did Walter earn in his Navy career, how much did he send home, and how much of that still remained at discharge?

Walter's pay gradually increased as he rose in rank from seaman, ($72/month) to PhM1/c, ($135/ month). Factors like time in service and assignment also affected pay. My best guess puts Walter's total pay during his almost four years in service at about $4,500.

In his letters Walter wrote a lot about money, how much he spent and how much something cost. His own spending habits were different than most corpsmen. He spent nothing on alcohol or cigarettes or gambling. For himself, I am sure he spent less than a dollar a day, and many days he spent nothing at all. He will spend enough for a good pen or decent watch, and he will spend more on gifts for family members. The only times he approached extravagance were his gifts for Myrtle. I estimate his total spending for his entire time in service at between $1,000 and $1,500.

So how much, if any, of the $3,000 to $3,500 he sent home, did Myrtle keep? Again, I am indebted to David, who was on the ranch for the war's duration. He remembers that Myrtle and Al spent almost nothing on 'store bought' food. During the Depression, which was barely behind them, they had existed on what they could grow and little else. Another helpful measure of their spending is a 1942 ledger I found among Dad's papers. Among expenses recorded in this ledger, I found a purchase labeled 'tobacco' which showed the amount as five cents. I believe David is correct when he suggests Myrtle may have saved all the money Walter sent home.

Epilogue

Post-traumatic stress disorder became an acknowledged medical diagnosis in 1980. Previously known as 'shell shock' or 'combat fatigue,' PTSD is a mental health condition that can occur after experiencing or witnessing a shocking, terrifying, or dangerous event. Common symptoms include flashbacks, nightmares, difficulty sleeping, and depression. The symptoms can persist or worsen and interfere with day-to-day functioning. Treatment is often critical, and without it the patient may deteriorate.

Walter's PTSD likely resulted from the many times he witnessed sudden death and injury on the battlefield. He suffered physical trauma when he was knocked down and deafened by incoming artillery blasts. He retrieved wounded and dead Marines while under fire, some whom he knew and considered friends. With no time for grieving, these memories piled up and led to uncontrollable emotions. As long as Walter kept those memories buried, he functioned well, but if some event made him recall those past experiences then the nightmares and flashbacks grew worse. For years Walter managed his PTSD by working himself to physical exhaustion. When he was no longer able to do this, his symptoms worsened.

In 1991, eleven years after Mom died, Walter married Lee Masters. His nightmares and flashbacks persisted, and he was unable to hide his symptoms from Lee. He resisted counseling and 'talk therapy' for what he felt was a good reason – talking about his experiences and feelings seemed to make things worse. He needed an alternative treatment. He found Neurofeedback.

Psychology Today describes neurofeedback as a therapy "… that provides immediate feedback from a computer-based program that assesses a client's brainwave activity…" and then uses sound or visual signals to retrain the brain. Fortunately, Walter connected with Bruce Ammons, a local psychologist who specialized in neurofeedback, and his PTSD became manageable.

PTSD aside, the war did not alter the basic values Walter learned from Myrtle. Helping others was an article of faith, leavened with self-interest. If a neighbor broke his leg and couldn't put up hay, the Dodds would pitch in. If a family living nearby lost their cabin to a fire, their children would be taken in for the duration of the emergency. Besides being 'the Christian thing to do' it was a sort of savings account, ready to be drawn on in a possible future if misfortune struck the Dodd family.

One Sunday, when I was about ten, we were at church when a broke-down cowboy showed up and approached Dad. After the service, the man, who was shaky and needed a shave, rode home with us. After dinner, Dad took him outside to a patch of bull thistles and handed him a grub hoe. After a couple hours of chopping, Dad drove the man back to town and (as I learned much later) gave him enough cash for a bottle, perhaps in memory of Lloyd DeVore.

Walter wanted to die at home and in 2016, a week after he turned 98, he succeeded. He was honored with full military honors at graveside, complete with honor guard, draping of the casket, folding and presentation of the flag, taps and a three-volley salute. In his letters, Walter always maintained a healthy skepticism regarding military pomp, writing, "… it is always said by the boys that know, the medals don't mean much unless the true facts are known." I think that later in life, Walter put aside his self-effacing modesty and admitted, perhaps even to himself, that he had acted above and beyond ordinary duty and did, in fact, deserve the medals he received. Walter certainly never claimed to be a hero, but when he repeatedly placed duty over his own desires, his actions provided the proof.

My true facts are these: Walter treated me better than I deserved, taught me more than I realized, and loved me without judgement. It is a joy for me to pay tribute to him, a hero unaware.

PGIL2021USA